The
FEISTY STITCHER

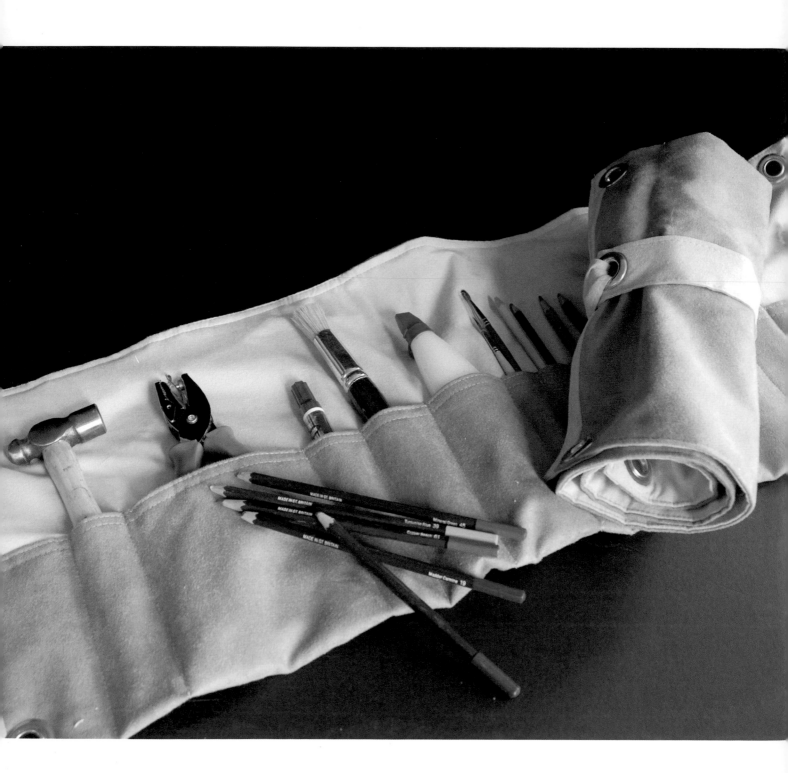

The FEISTY STITCHER

Sewing Projects with Attitude

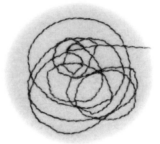

Susan Wasinger

LARK
CRAFTS

A DIVISION OF STERLING PUBLISHING CO., INC.

New York / London

746
WAS

1-11-11

Senior Editor:
VALERIE SHRADER

Copy Editor:
JANE HARRIS WOODSIDE

Design, Photography, and
Illustration:
SUSAN WASINGER

Library of Congress Cataloging-in-Publication Data

Wasinger, Susan.
   The feisty stitcher : sewing projects with attitude / Susan Wasinger.
          p. cm.
   Includes index.
   ISBN 978-1-60059-465-6 (pb-pbk. with flaps : alk. paper)
1. Textile crafts. 2. Sewing. I. Title.
   TT699.W39 2010
   746--dc22

                                    2009015553

10 9 8 7 6 5 4 3 2

Published by Lark Crafts, A Division of
Sterling Publishing Co., Inc.
387 Park Avenue South, New York, NY 10016

Text and Photography © 2009, Susan Wasinger

Distributed in Canada by Sterling Publishing, c/o Canadian Manda Group,
165 Dufferin Street, Toronto, Ontario, Canada M6K 3H6

Distributed in the United Kingdom by GMC Distribution Services,
Castle Place, 166 High Street, Lewes, East Sussex, England BN7 1XU

Distributed in Australia by Capricorn Link (Australia) Pty Ltd.,
P.O. Box 704, Windsor, NSW 2756 Australia

If you have questions or comments about this book, please contact:
Lark Crafts
67 Broadway
Asheville, NC 28801
828-253-0467

Manufactured in China

ISBN 978-1-60059-465-6

For information about custom editions, special sales, premium and corporate purchases, please contact Sterling Special Sales Department at 800-805-5489 or specialsales@sterlingpub.com.

For information about desk and examination copies available to college and university professors, requests must be submitted to academic@larkbooks.com. Our complete policy can be found at www.larkcrafts.com.

LARK
CRAFTS

This book is dedicated to my miraculous children, Camille and Rainer Wasinger, who by their very nature and existence are a constant source of inspiration and optimism and hope.

May the things you do in your life bring you joy!

The FEISTY STITCHER

contents

Tips & Techniques • 9   Patterns • 124   Index • 128

Carry it!

Hit-the-Road BACKPACK --------------- 18

Oilcloth BIKE BAGS ------------------- 24

ART STUDIO On-a-Roll ---------------- 28

Enlightened MESSENGER BAG ---------- 32

T-Shirt MARKET BAG ------------------ 38

Wear it!

Fuzzy SLIPPER BOOTS ----------------- 44

Furry TRAPPER'S HAT ----------------- 50

Buttoned-Up BAUBLES ----------------- 56

Quick, Cute, Clever JACKET ----------- 60

Piece-ful EASY SCARF ---------------- 66

Nip & Tuck T-SHIRT ------------------ 70

Live with it!

Punched-Up LAMPSHADE --------------- 76

Barkcloth & Jute FLOOR CUSHIONS ------- 80

Snap-to-It STORAGE ------------------ 86

Ready-to-Roll MAT ------------------- 92

Upholstery Webbing BULLETIN BOARD ------ 96

Pile-it-On DENIM RUG ---------------- 100

Give it away!

Conical COIN PURSE ------------------ 104

Laminated FELT CASE ----------------- 108

Inner Tube DAY PLANNER -------------- 112

Sew-Green GIFT TAGS ----------------- 116

Selvage-Striped TOTE ---------------- 118

Uppity Seamsters Unite!

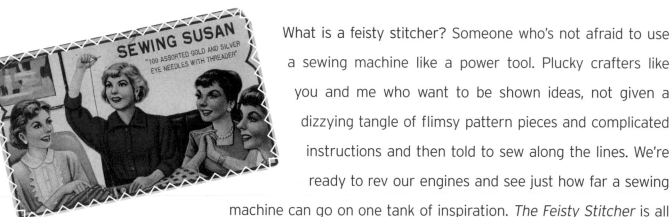

What is a feisty stitcher? Someone who's not afraid to use a sewing machine like a power tool. Plucky crafters like you and me who want to be shown ideas, not given a dizzying tangle of flimsy pattern pieces and complicated instructions and then told to sew along the lines. We're ready to rev our engines and see just how far a sewing machine can go on one tank of inspiration. *The Feisty Stitcher* is all about trying new things: new fabrics, new hardware, new techniques to make fun, modern projects that are the caffeinated versions of the fussy stuff your great aunt thought you should sew. From grommets to French seams to funky hardware, these new materials and techniques may look advanced and complex, but there really isn't much to them once you break it down. And the Tips and Techniques section that follows does just that. It demystifies feisty sewing and gives you an arsenal of simple and solid knowledge that puts you on the road to creative independence. Throughout the book, the savvy/fearless/fabulous projects feature color how-to photos, nifty illustrations, and pithy text with a show-me-AND-tell-me style that eases you into the adventure of sewing. Armed with nothing but your trusty old machine and a basic tool kit, you're ready to venture out where few seamsters have gone before. Sew a set of snap-together stacking bins to store all your stuff. Let the faux fur fly to whip up a deliciously chic version of a trapper's hat. Or brave wildly hip oilcloth to make the coolest bike bags on two wheels. Feisty sewing isn't for sissies! So ladies and gentlemen, start your machines, power up your imagination, and start thinking outside the sewing box.

Tips & Techniques

MACHINE TALK • Don't think you need a fancy machine to sew these projects. Despite the brazen feistiness of this book's projects, I created them on a 20-year-old Bernina and a retro Singer from the 1950s, both of them ordinary workhorse machines designed with the well-behaved home seamstress in mind. But the truth is, these machines are powerful tools that can pierce a lot of layers of fabric without popping a bobbin. That's all you need: a trusty machine, one that's ready for an adventure and is brave enough to seam together something completely unexpected.

ALL STITCHED UP • The projects in this book require few special stitches. Your machine needs to be able to do a straight stitch and a zigzag—really, that's it. Granted, one project uses an overcast stitch, but in a pinch, even this one can be finished using a traditional zigzag.

straight stitch
zigzag stitch
overcast stitch

IN THE THICK OF IT • It's scary to sew through a lot of layers. The machine's engine sometimes complains, or the needle stops with an unhealthy-sounding "thunk." It might seem that the needle just can't go through, but the truth is, these machines are designed to handle a lot. If you follow a few simple rules, they'll sail smoothly over almost anything. Here's how to slog through the tough stuff:

1 Slow down It's all about keeping the needle on top in sync with the fabric feeding through down below. Slowing down helps them operate together smoothly. Sometimes you'll need to keep some tension on the fabric to help feed it through under the presser foot.

2 Pull the pins I'm generally a pinner, not a baster, and I have occasionally been known to ride roughshod over a pin or two. (Naughty, naughty.) But on layers of heavy fabric, you're almost guaranteed to break the needle if you try to sew over a pin. In some cases, it might be smarter to try basting the seam to hold the fabrics in place while you sew. But if, like me, you are an insistent pinner, just be sure you take them out before the needle finds them.

3 Keep it on the level When you're blithely sewing along and suddenly hit a seam that's double the original thickness, your presser foot tries to climb up over the lump—and trouble starts. When the presser foot is no longer level, you risk having your needle hit metal (resulting in a teeth-rattling break). To avoid this, have a stack of fabric or cardboard handy to slip under the presser foot's back edge so it stays even. Some machines have an attachment for this purpose.

Keep the presser foot level.

UNUSUAL MATERIALS • Life is too short to play it safe. Don't be afraid to try a material you've never used before; it may have qualities that actually make it easier to work with. For instance, extra-thick felt, patent leather, and innertube rubber don't fray, making it easy to finish edges or even leave the raw edges exposed. Other fabrics lend a jaunty, tough-guy charm that gives your project character and attitude even before you sew a stitch, like thick cotton canvas, brawny denim, hard-wearing upholstery fabrics, wipe-able oilcloth, and faux suede. And please recycle! Try repurposing old sweaters, the vintage barkcloth from old curtains, or even a fabric you make from fused plastic bags. They're the perfect starting points for projects that are eco-friendly *and* fashion conscious. Dig a little deeper at the fabric store, push out of your comfort zone—and sewing will never be the same.

FAT THREAD • Most projects in this book are sewn with regular old thread, the stuff you can get just about anywhere in a dazzling rainbow of colors. But on some projects, a heavyweight thread that makes an obvious and dramatic line of stitching is just the ticket. For topstitching on heavy fabrics, for machine appliqué, or anywhere else you really want to call attention to your needle-work, this thread provides an extra dimension to home sewing. Available in only a slightly more limited range of colors than regular thread, heavyweight thread works better when used with a larger topstitch needle (see page 13). Heavier threads might require you to adjust your machine's thread tension to make the stitch look good on both the front and the backside. Experiment, and consult your owner's manual to get the tension just right.

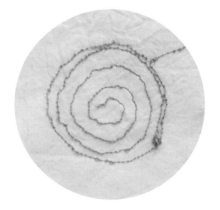

MACHINE APPLIQUÉ • Apply a little creativity to a scrap of fabric and fire up your sewing machine to make appliqués with a new, no-holds-barred attitude. Yeah, it can still be cute, but it's not teddy bear cute. It's a frayed-around-the-edges, little-bit-impish brand of cute. Let all the stitches show, make it funky on purpose, and don't try too hard.

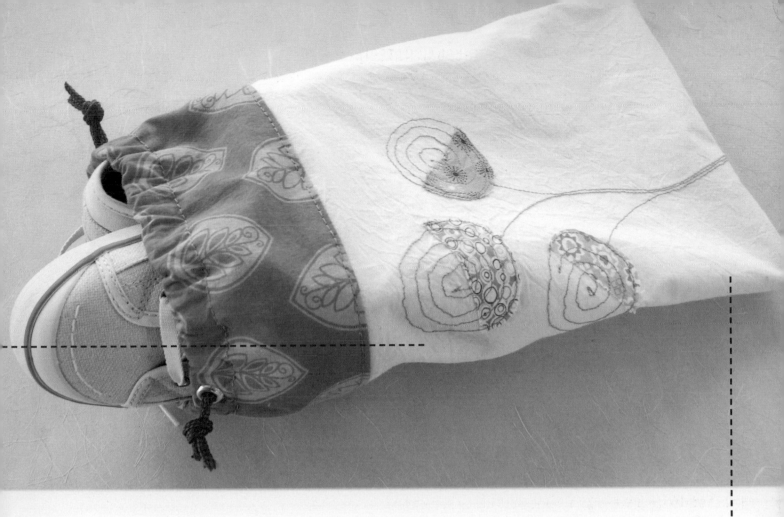

FRENCH SEAM • Almost all the projects in this book use a plain old seam: the simple right-sides-together, sew-a-straight-stitch-1/2-inch (1.3 cm)-from-the-edge seam. But there's another type that's useful to learn because it creates a seam that's guaranteed not to ravel and makes a project look good from both the inside and the outside. It's called a French seam. It takes a little longer to do, but not much, and it's super easy.

You'll need to cut a seam allowance wider for a French seam: just add a 1/4 inch (0.6 cm) extra to any side of your cut pieces that has a seam. Start with wrong sides together. Sew a line of stitching 1/4 inch (0.6 cm) in from the edge. Trim the edges to about 1/8 inch (0.3 cm) away from the stitch line. Now fold the fabric along the stitch line, putting RIGHT sides together and encasing the raw edges within the fold. Crease along the seam and pin. To make your actual seam, stitch a line down about 1/4 inch to 3/8 inch (0.6 to .95 cm) from the edge. The raw edge is now beautifully and quite professionally finished.

Sew narrow seam with wrong sides together.

Open fabric and trim seam edges to 1/8" (0.3cm).

Fold fabric over seam so right sides are together, sew another seam to finish.

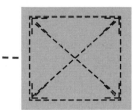

X-REINFORCMENT • This is a simple-to-sew, hard-to-beat way to attach a strap or reinforce a fold-back connection. It looks good and is guaranteed to carry its weight. Sew the top line of stitching first and then the bottom. Next sew the diagonals, and finish by adding the sides. Use a bar tack—backstitch a few stitches—at each line's beginning and end.

GROMMETS • Grommets have two pieces: the actual grommet—the piece with the post—and the ring or washer that fits over it. The grommet is on the finished outside; the washer, on the inside. Grommet kits contain an anvil, which has a groove that fits the grommet's front contour, and a punch, which fits inside the post and squashes it down into the ring when hit with a hammer. That's what sets the grommet. Always make a test run on a scrap first to get the hang of it.

HARDWARE • The notions department at your local fabric store has some interesting items that can give your projects an industrial vibe. For example, take a second look at big metal zippers, magnetic purse closures, and button blanks to cover your own buttons. But don't confine yourself to sewing notions. Hardware stores have plenty of stuff that can add character and attitude to your sewing projects. Try hasps, carabiners, large washers, steel or brass rings, or cinch buckles—just to name a few.

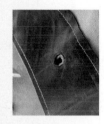

Mark and cut the hole in the fabric so it's large enough for the grommet post.

Insert the grommet post through the hole from the fabric's right side. Turn the fabric over, and put the ring or washer on the post.

SPECIALTY SEWING MACHINE NEEDLES • Leather needles (also known as cutting needles) are extra sturdy needles with a cutting tip that pierces through to make even stitches in tough fabrics. They're available at most big-box fabric stores, or wherever sewing machines are sold. Not just for leather, they're a must for innertube rubber. For heavy fabrics like denim, canvas, or multiple layers of cotton duck, this needle helps keep stitches from skipping. Another useful needle type is the topstitch needle. It has an extra large hole and a deeper groove to fit the fatter, heavier topstitch threads.

Place the anvil under the grommet and then position the punch so that it goes through the ring. Hit the punch a few times with the hammer to set.

INSPIRATION FROM EVERYDAY ITEMS
• Look for inspiration in the simplest artifacts of daily life. A regular envelope can become the template for a business card case, a change purse, or, on a larger scale, a perfect portfolio. To make the portfolios opposite, I dismantled a birthday card envelope to cut out the shape. Other everyday things that might inspire a project: paper bags, button-and-string envelopes, even a cardboard box (the Snap-to-It Storage bins on page 86 used a template from just such a humble box).

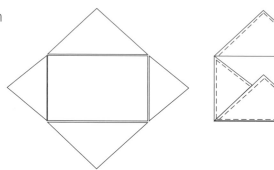

IT'S A SNAP

Push the snap front through the fabric, using a pencil eraser to force the fabric to the base of the prongs.

Place the ring on the prongs, with the protruding center up.

Place a spool of thread over the ring so the hole in the center of the spool is over the ring. Hit firmly with a hammer to set.

Repeat to set on the other flap, with the nipple on the top and the backing ring going up and through.

TOPSTITCHING
• A lot of projects really benefit from topstitching; this gives them a more professional, crisp, natty finish. Generally, topstitching is done fairly close to the fabric's edge, about $1/8$ inch (0.3 cm) in, but you can vary the distance according to what you find pleasing; use a matching or contrasting thread. For extra emphasis, topstitch in heavy-duty thread. You can also do a double row of topstitching, like you see on the seams of jeans; usually one row is $1/8$ inch (0.3 cm) in, and the second is about $3/8$ inch (.95 cm) from the edge.

CRAZY STITCHING
• I'm a big believer in letting your stitches show. Sometimes I like to sort of "doodle" on the fabric with stitching. I pretty much always do it freehand, just trusting the gods of randomness to make something pleasing. This is another situation where it's important to sew slowly so you can guide your fabric—turning it this way and that—to let the lines meander smoothly. Radiating lines of straight stitching can also look fetching, as can a grid or circles or spirals. Get out a scrap of fabric to experiment on first, then start playing. (But be sure to keep your fingers out of harm's way as you buzz around.)

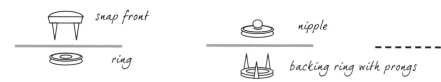

snap front

ring

nipple

backing ring with prongs

SNAPS AND CLOSURES
• There's something about snaps that's so beguiling. Maybe it's that satisfying click when they come together. Snaps come in all sizes and colors these days, which makes them as much fun as buttons to design with. The process for setting the snaps is fairly simple; some don't even require any special tools, though you can also buy inexpensive sets that contain the snaps *and* the setting tools in one. I also love magnetic closures, the kind that come on purses and bags. Again, there's that wonderfully satisfying click! These are really easy to set, as they require no tools at all: they have prongs that fold over like brads. Do give them a try.

carry it!

Hit-the-Road Backpack

Oilcloth Bike Bags

Art Studio On-a-Roll • Enlightened Messenger Bag • T-Shirt Market Bag

EASE LEVEL:	breezy intermediate
TIME REQUIREMENT:	a couple of hours
COST:	a week of lattes
UNEXPECTED MATERIALS:	eco-felt

You can strap this flexible bag on your back, grab the top handle, or pull the straps through the handle for an over-the-shoulder sling.

Hit-the-Road BACKPACK

Layer on the style with this natty little backpack that's all about the edge. Humble felt in no-nonsense industrial gray gets a boost from layers of color and lots of stitching. Here the palette takes its cue from asphalt and the lines on the highway, but you can draw on your own inspiration to make a pack that's the perfect companion for all your adventures.

Materials & Tools

- basic tool kit (see page 9)

- 3 pieces of wool, wool blend felt, or eco-felt* in three different colors, each 5/8 yard (57.2 cm) long

- compass or household objects for tracing circles

- covered button, 1 1/2 inches (3.8 cm) wide (see pages 56-57 to make your own)

  Eco-felt is felt made from recycled plastic water bottles. It is dense and cushy, and feels more like natural fiber felt than like flimsy acrylic craft felt. It is available in a rainbow of colors at most big-box fabric stores.

Check out page 56-57 for instructions on how to make these cool felt-covered buttons.

Make the cut

Cut three layers (one of each color) of every piece.

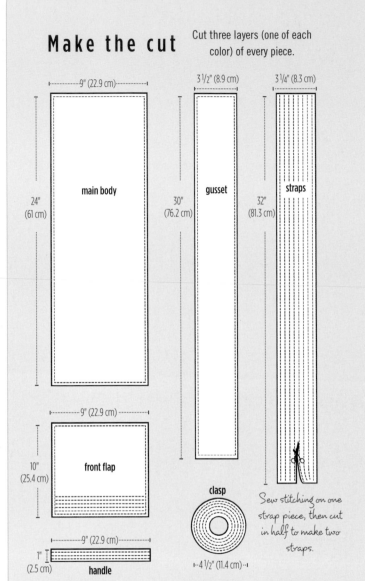

9" (22.9 cm)

24" (61 cm) — main body

3 1/2" (8.9 cm)

30" (76.2 cm) — gusset

3 1/4" (8.3 cm)

32" (81.3 cm) — straps

Sew stitching on one strap piece, then cut in half to make two straps.

9" (22.9 cm)

10" (25.4 cm) — front flap

clasp

4 1/2" (11.4 cm)

9" (22.9 cm)

1" (2.5 cm) — handle

Each piece for this bag is made up of three layers of felt fabric sewn together. For the main body, the gusset, and the front flap, just sew around the perimeter to hold the pieces together. For the handle, the circular clasp, and the strap, multiple lines of stitching reinforce and decorate the layers. To make the two straps, one piece is cut and sewn, then cut straight down the middle.

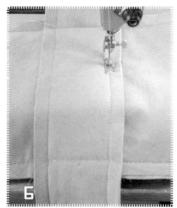

Here's how

1 Cut out all necessary pieces, as per cutting instructions at left. Stack the three layers for each piece and pin. For the main body, gusset, and front flap pieces, machine-sew around the perimeter about $1/2$ inch (1.3 cm) from the edge.

2 & 3 For the straps, layer together the three colors, and sew one line of stitching about $1/2$ inch (1.3 cm) from the edge. Sew subsequent lines $1/4$ inch (0.6 cm) apart across the strap's width. Cut between the two center lines to make the two straps. Trim the raw edge to about $1/8$ inch (0.3 cm) from the stitching.

4 Begin assembly by laying the gusset right side up. Next, place the main body piece on top so it's perpendicular to the gusset. Make sure the main piece is centered on the gusset both top to bottom and side to side. Slip about 1 inch (2.5 cm) of one strap end under the side of the main piece where it overlaps the gusset, as shown. Repeat on the main piece's other side.

5 Pin the strap in place and sew the three pieces (main body, strap end, gusset) together about $1/2$ inch (1.3 cm) from the main piece edge. Repeat on the other side.

6 Turn the whole construction over. To define the bag's bottom edge, pin and then sew the gusset to the main body with a line of stitching $1/2$ inch (1.3 cm) from the gusset edge, as shown. Sew along both the front and the back gusset edges

7 To make the fold smoother and less lumpy in later steps, clip a small triangle at the corner where the side of the bag will fold up. Repeat on the bottom's remaining three corners.

8 Flip over the whole piece, and sew a line of stitching about $1/4$ inch (0.6 cm) over from the seam you sewed in step 5. This stitching should extend between the two lines of stitching from step 6. Trim the fabric about $1/8$ inch (0.3 cm) from the stitching.
(continued on page 22)

9

10

11

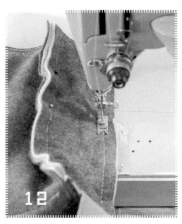

12

13

14

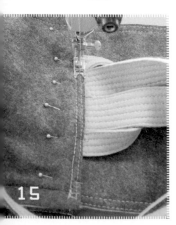

15

16

Here's how (continued)

9, 10, & 11 To form the backpack, start with the piece facedown on a flat surface. Fold up the main piece's front and the side gusset at the corner. Bring these two edges together (wrong sides facing) and pin. Work your way up the seam, making sure the edges meet evenly. Repeat on the other three corners.

12 Sew the side seams about 1/2 inch (1.3 cm) from the edge. For the bag's front, sew these seams from the bottom to the top. In the back, leave the top 2 to 3 inches (5.1 or 7.6 cm) open for now. You'll sew these together later when adding the flap to the backpack.

13 Layer, sew, and trim the front flap and the handle pieces.

14 Assemble the flap, handle, and straps at the back of the bag, as shown: The flap edge goes about 2 inches (5.1 cm) deep into the bag. The strap ends go in about 1 inch (2.5 cm) deep, positioned so they're right next to each other at the center of the back. Next, place the first handle end about 5/8 inch (1.6 cm) into the bag and just to the left of the straps. Now pass the handle under the straps, and tuck the other handle end in just to the right of the straps. This will put the handle in front of the straps when you're looking at the front of the bag. Make sure that neither strap is twisted and that the lining color is out. Pin all layers in place.

15 Sew through all the layers about 1/2 inch (1.3 cm) from the edge to secure the various pieces. This line will be along the stitching you sewed in step 1. Sew a second line of topstitching about 1/4 inch (0.6 cm) away. (See Topstitching on page 14.) Once the flap is in place, finish the vertical seam from step 12.

16 Time to topstitch and trim. Sew a second line of stitching on all side seams about 1/4 inch (0.6 cm) from the original seams. Do the same around the top edge of the bag. Trim back all seams evenly to about 1/8 inch (0.3 cm) from the stitching to really show off the layers of color and to tidy up the backpack. Extra-sharp scissors really help here.

An even simpler clasp for closing the backpack is a narrow loop of doubled felt.

17 To make the clasp, use a circular object to draw two circles, one about 4¹/₂ inches (11.4 cm) in diameter and the second about 1¹/₂ inches (3.8 cm) in diameter. (Hint: Raid your kitchen cabinets for the perfect-sized objects.) Or use a compass if you prefer.

18 Sew along the marked lines through all layers of felt. Then sew another line of stitching centered between the two. Finally, sew one more line between the existing lines until you have five lines of concentric stitching. With sharp scissors, cut a circle out of the middle about ¹/₈ inch (0.3 cm) from the stitching and trim the outer edge of the circle to neaten up the clasp.

19 Buy or create a button about 1¹/₂ inches (3.8 cm) wide. Position the stitched circle in the flap's center so that one-half of the circle hangs below the bottom edge of the flap. Stitch along the bottom row of topstitching on the flap to attach the circle clasp. Trim away the other half of the clasp if you'd like.

20 Using the flap as your guide, mark the spot where the button should be on the backpack. Sew the button into place with a needle and doubled thread.

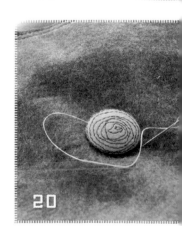

EASE LEVEL: lots simpler than they look

TIME REQUIREMENT: not quite an hour each

COST: less than store-bought

UNEXPECTED MATERIALS: retro oilcloth available online

Oilcloth BIKE BAGS

They're jaunty little bags—perfect for your sweet cruiser, vintage Sting-Ray, or tough-guy single speed. They're the ultimate ride for your keys, cell phone, wallet, lock, or whatever else you need when traveling light. The bright oilcloth—available in a dizzying array of retro prints—adds a free-wheelin' attitude. Hook-and-loop tape makes them easy to take off, so at the end of the road, whisk them away, and they'll be your purse for the day.

Materials & Tools

- basic tool kit (see page 9)

FOR RED BAG:

- $1/2$ yard (45.7 cm) of red floral oilcloth

- 1 yard (0.9 m) of tan fold-over braid or bias braid, $5/8$ inch (1.6 cm) wide

- 2 hair ties in black or color to match bag

- 2 buttons

- 1 yard (0.9 m) of hook-and-loop tape in red, $1/2$ inch (1.3 cm) wide

FOR BLUE BAG:

- $1/2$ yard (45.7 cm) of blue floral oilcloth

- 1 yard (0.9 m) of red fold-over braid or bias braid, $5/8$ inch (1.6 cm) wide (I used jute and cotton braid)

- 1 hair tie in black or color to match bag

- 2 buttons

- 1 yard (0.9 m) of hook-and-loop tape in red, $1/2$ inch (1.3 cm) wide

Make the cut

Put it together

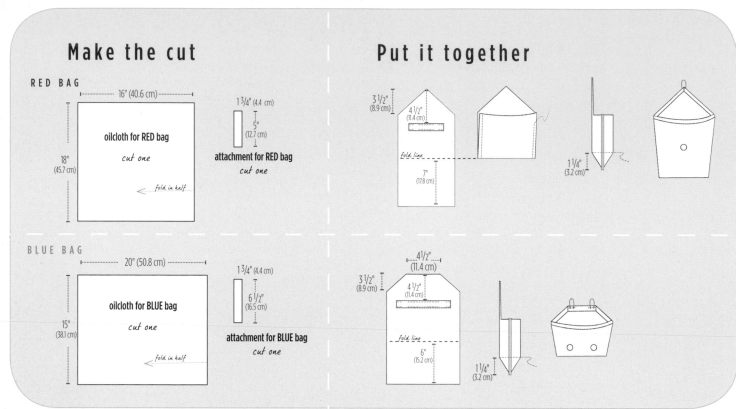

RED BAG

16" (40.6 cm)

18" (45.7 cm)

oilcloth for RED bag

cut one

← *fold in half*

1 3/4" (4.4 cm)

5" (12.7 cm)

attachment for RED bag
cut one

3 1/2" (8.9 cm)

4 1/2" (11.4 cm)

fold line

7" (17.8 cm)

1 1/4" (3.2 cm)

BLUE BAG

20" (50.8 cm)

15" (38.1 cm)

oilcloth for BLUE bag

cut one

← *fold in half*

1 3/4" (4.4 cm)

6 1/2" (16.5 cm)

attachment for BLUE bag
cut one

4 1/2" (11.4 cm)

3 1/2" (8.9 cm)

4 1/2" (11.4 cm)

fold line

6" (15.2 cm)

1 1/4" (3.2 cm)

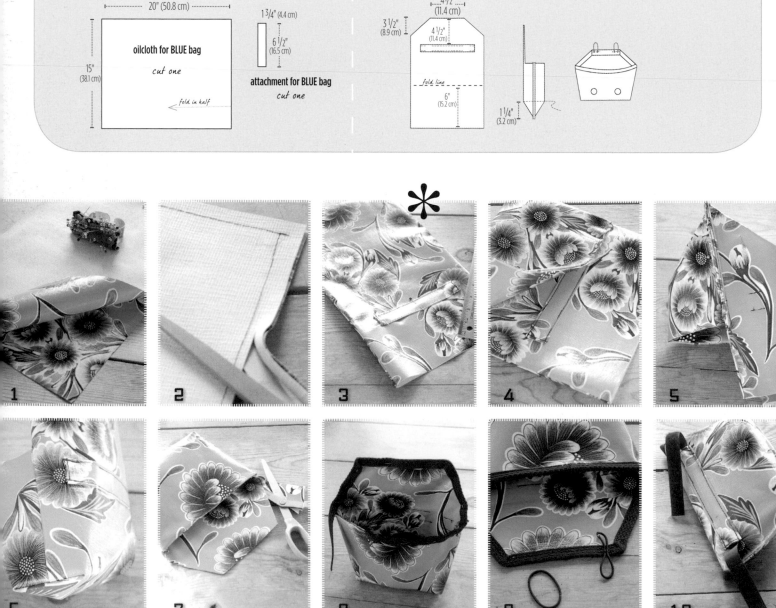

1

2

3

4

5

6

7

8

9

10

Here's how

1 Cut out the two necessary pieces for the bag you've chosen, as per instructions at left. Fold the large main rectangle in half with right sides together, as shown on diagram. Pin and sew 1/2 inch (1.3 cm) along the open side and bottom. Leave the top open.

2 Trim the seam to about 1/8 inch (0.3 cm).

3 Turn the rectangle right-side out and lay flat. Follow the instructions at right to make the attachment strap for the bag. (The strap will allow you to use hook-and-loop tape to attach the bag to any type of seat or handlebar.) Position this strap on the bag 4 1/2 inches (11.4 cm) from the top as specified in the diagram at left, and sew into place, (through both layers) as shown in the instructions at right.

4 With the sewn strap facing up, fold the bottom of the bag up the amount specified in the diagram for the bag you're making. Pin both sides, and sew a 1/2-inch (1.3 cm) seam. This will create a finished seam that will make for a neat interior.

5 & 6 To form the bag bottom, fold the side of the bag down to a point as shown and pin. Sew a horizontal seam 1 1/4 inches (3.2 cm) up from the point to make a bottom gusset. Repeat on the other side. Turn the bag right side out.

7 Measure, mark, and cut the angles in the bag flap, as specified in the diagram.

8 Starting on the inside, place the fold-over braid or bias tape over the raw edges around the "mouth" of the bag, centering the tape on the edge. Pin as you go. Ease the tape around corners. Fold the end of the tape over itself, and overlap the beginning slightly to make a nice start/finish. Pin, baste, then sew into place close to the edge.

9 For the blue bag, position the two colored hair ties on the bag's inside lip, each one about 1/2 inch (1.3 cm) in from the side, as shown. Sew in place with a satin stitch or tight zigzag. Close the flap and hand sew the buttons on the front so the hair tie stretches a bit to reach them. If you're making the red bag, hand sew one button right at the point in the front flap. Loop the hair tie over this button and knot it securely around the button's base. Hand sew the second button on the bag's front so the hair tie has to stretch a little to reach it.

10 Use hook-and-loop tape to attach the bag to your bike. For vertical loop applications, cut two pieces of hook tape, each 9 inches (22.9 cm) long. On one end of each piece, sew a 2-inch (5.1 cm) piece of loop tape to the WRONG side of the hook tape. This will allow you to close it. (For horizontal applications, cut loop tape 18 inches [45.7 cm] and add 4 inches [10.2 cm] of hook tape to the end).

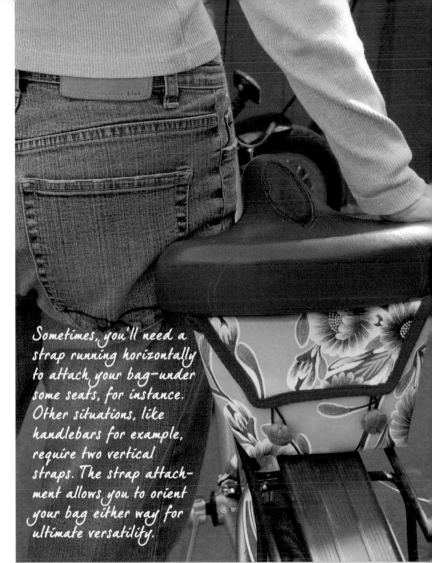

Sometimes, you'll need a strap running horizontally to attach your bag—under some seats, for instance. Other situations, like handlebars for example, require two vertical straps. The strap attachment allows you to orient your bag either way for ultimate versatility.

1"
(2.5 cm)

1/2"
(1.3 cm)

attachment strap
Cut to size specified. Fold both the ends and the sides in 1/4 inch (0.6 cm) and pin. Sew all the way around the perimeter about 1/8 inch (0.3 cm) from edge. To sew the strap onto the bag, sew along the top and bottom edges to make a sleeve; beginning at a point 1/2 inch (1.3 cm) in from the end of each strap, leave a 1-inch (2.5 cm) gap in the stitching.

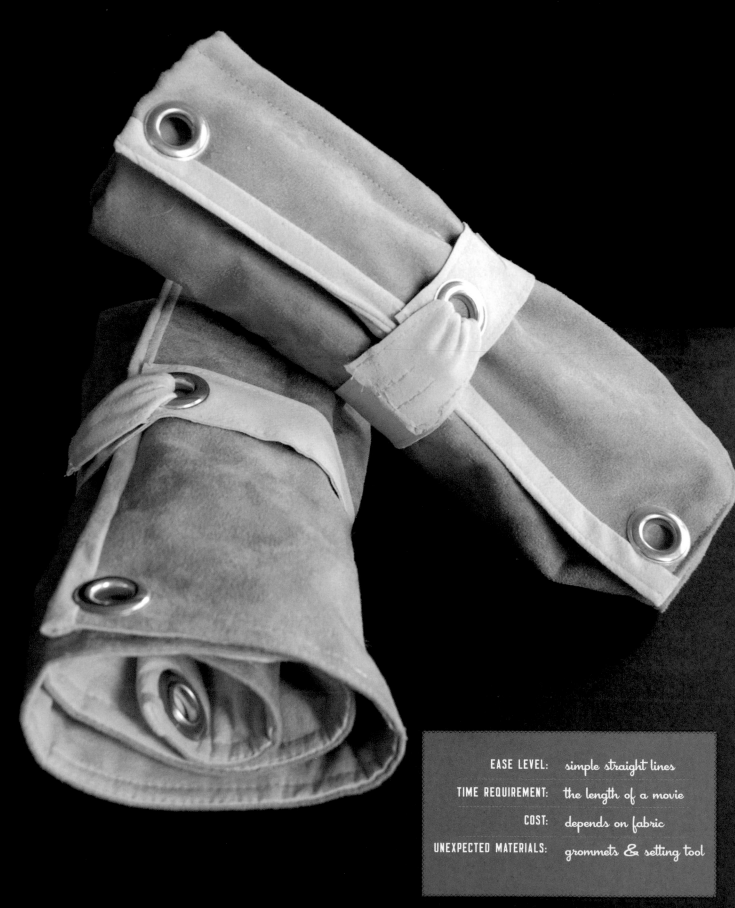

EASE LEVEL:	*simple straight lines*
TIME REQUIREMENT:	*the length of a movie*
COST:	*depends on fabric*
UNEXPECTED MATERIALS:	*grommets & setting tool*

ART STUDIO On-a-Roll

Ever get the hankering to sew on the go? This luxe, microsuede tool roll gives your favorite implements first-class accommodations. It's a great way to store your tools for paper crafting, sewing, needlework, drawing, painting—whatever. When you're ready to put them to use, just hang up the roll by the grommets and carabiners, and make any room in the house your own crafting studio.

Materials & Tools

- basic tool kit (see page 9)
- 1/2 yard (45.7 cm) each of outer fabric and lining (I used easy-to-work, buttery-soft microsuede in tan and yellow)
- iron-on interfacing
- iron
- 5 large grommets
- grommet setting tool and hammer
- hook-and-loop tape
- carabiners for hanging

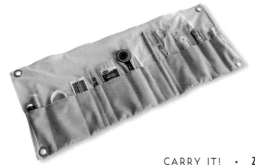

Make the cut

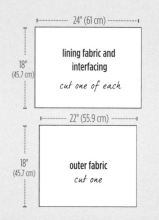

24" (61 cm)

lining fabric and interfacing

cut one of each

18" (45.7 cm)

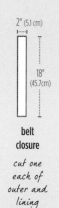

2" (5.1 cm)

18" (45.7 cm)

belt closure

cut one each of outer and lining fabric

22" (55.9 cm)

outer fabric

cut one

18" (45.7 cm)

Put it together

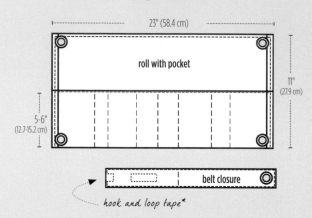

23" (58.4 cm)

roll with pocket

11" (27.9 cm)

5–6" (12.7-15.2 cm)

belt closure

hook and loop tape*

＊ Cut two pieces of hook-and-loop tape: a hook piece about 1/2 inch (1.3 cm) long and a loop piece about 1 1/2 inches (3.8 cm) long. Attach the tape on the yellow lining piece of the closure. Sew the hook tape right on the end; sew the loop piece about 2 to 3 inches (5.1 to 7.6 cm) from the end.

Hang up your tool roll, and make any room an instant craft studio.
Carabiners are the perfect piece of hardware for the job (get them at your local
hardware store or any place that sells rock-climbing gear). Plus the bottom grommets on your roll give you another place to clip on extra tools of the trade!

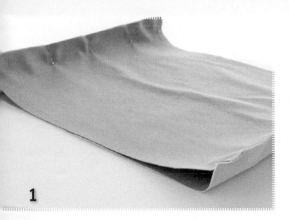

1

2

3

4

5

6

7

Here's how

1 & 2 Cut out all necessary pieces of the outer fabric, the lining, and the interfacing, as per cutting instructions at left. Iron the interfacing to the wrong side of the lining, following manufacturer's instructions. With right sides together, pin the outer fabric to the lining, centering the outer fabric on the lining side to side and matching the edges top to bottom. Sew $1/2$-inch (1.3 cm) side seams. Because the outer fabric is narrower than the lining, a bit of the lining will wrap to the outside, creating a colorful edging after the side seams are sewn. Trim the seams to make them less bulky; cut the outer fabric (tan) to about $1/4$-inch (0.6 cm) and the interfaced lining fabric (yellow) to $1/8$-inch (0.3 cm).

3 & 4 Make sure the edging is even on both sides. With right sides still together, pin and stitch a seam along the top and bottom edge of the piece, leaving about 3 inches (7.6 cm) open along the bottom seam to turn the fabric. Trim the

seams, and clip the corners. Turn the fabric, and hand sew the hole closed. Topstitch about $1/8$ inch (0.3 cm) from the edge on the top and bottom edge. (See Topstitching on page 14.) Do a second row of topstitching (as shown) if you'd like. Then sew along the edge adjacent to the contrasting yellow border.

5 Turn up the bottom edge of the piece about 5 to 6 inches (12.7 to 15.2 cm) to form the pocket, and pin in place, making sure that the sides line up. Sew the side edges along the same line as the topstitching in step 1. (You can add a second row wherever you've topstitched for a gutsier look.) Measure and mark the individual compartments vertically on the pocket. Use a variety of widths—from 1 inch (2.5 cm) to about 3 or $3 1/2$ inches (7.6 to 8.9 cm)—so the pockets work for all kinds of tools and materials. Draw these pocket separator lines, and then sew along them. Be sure to reinforce the top edge with about $1/2$ inch (1.3

cm) of backtacking (backstitch over the stitching, then forward stitch).

6 Add the grommets to the four corners of the piece, following manufacturer's instructions. (Also see Grommets on page 13.)

7 To make the belt closure for the roll, take the two belt pieces (to which you've attached the hook-and-loop tape), and topstitch them together along the perimeter, wrong sides facing, about $1/8$ inch (0.3 cm) from the edge. (My micro-suede was completely non-fraying, but if yours is prone to ravel, you can add a seam allowance to these pieces, sew it right sides together, then turn it to create finished edges.) Add a grommet at one end. Position the belt (with hook-and-loop tape side up) equidistant from the top and bottom of the roll so that the grommet is tangent to the roll's edge (as shown). Pin, then secure with a line of stitching that follows the nearest vertical pocket seam.

EASE LEVEL:	dedicated intermediate

TIME REQUIREMENT:	one lazy Sunday

COST:	virtually free

UNEXPECTED MATERIALS:	trash and hardware

Enlightened MESSENGER BAG

Can your sewing machine save the planet? Sure it can—well, a little piece of it, anyway. This bag is made from the worst kind of plastic shopping bags: the flimsy ones that clog the landfills, find their way into our oceans, and take a thousand years to degrade. Fuse them together with your home iron to make a material that's tough, flexible, and graphically interesting. It's a messenger bag with a message.

Materials & Tools

- basic tool kit (see page 9)

- baking parchment

- 5 or so mostly white flimsy plastic grocery/shopping bags for the base material

- iron

- 5 or so bags with large lettering, nice colors, or quirky graphics on them (any weight bag will do)

- 5 or so of those colorful plastic bags the newspaper comes in

- compass or household objects for tracing circles

- 3 slide buckles, each 2 inches (5.1 cm), in metal, plastic, or wood

- magnetic purse fastener

- colorful 1/2-inch (1.3 cm) button

- 2-inch (5.1 cm) metal washer with a 1/4-inch (0.6 cm) center hole

Make the cut

Make a piece of fused plastic that measures about 28 x 48 inches (71.1 x 122 cm) to cut out the main, bottom/side, and strap pieces.

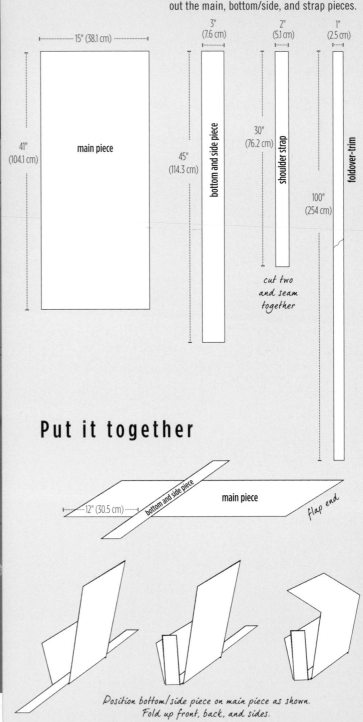

15" (38.1 cm)

41" (104.1 cm)

main piece

3" (7.6 cm)

45" (114.3 cm)

bottom and side piece

2" (5.1 cm)

30" (76.2 cm)

shoulder strap

cut two and seam together

1" (2.5 cm)

100" (254 cm)

foldover-trim

Put it together

12" (30.5 cm)

bottom and side piece

main piece

flap end

Position bottom/side piece on main piece as shown.
Fold up front, back, and sides.

Here's how

1 Do this in a well-ventilated room. It is best to practice on a small piece of fused plastic first to get the hang of it. Cover your ironing surface with the baking parchment. Cut the handles and the bottom off of a white plastic bag, and open the seam to make a plastic rectangle. Lay out several plastic pieces, letting them overlap a little, to create a large piece of plastic. Build up two or three layers, and then lay baking parchment on top. Move a hot, dry iron over the parchment, being sure to hold the iron in each place for a few seconds until you have gone over the entire surface. Let the fabric cool until the parchment crinkles off the surface. Check to see if the plastic is fused, and repeat if necessary. Keep layering and fusing until you have a piece about 28 x 48 inches (71.1 x 122 cm). Then add more layers as needed until your fabric is thick but still very flexible. Depending on the weight of your bags, three to five layers will probably be about right. Turn the whole thing over, and iron on the other side (still using the parchment to make sure iron doesn't touch plastic).

2 Cut out interesting lettering, graphics, or colors from plastic bags and iron them onto the surface. Pay special attention to decorating the area of fabric that will be your flap. Be sure to always sandwich the plastic between layers of parchment before you iron. This graphic layer will add more heft to your fabric; watch that it doesn't get too thick or stiff.

3 Use a long straightedge ruler to measure the main piece, bottom/side piece, and the straps. Mark them and cut. Keep the leftover scraps for later.

4 Cut long strips from the plastic newspaper bags (I used blue and green) to make the fold-over trim for the bag's contrasting edge. Three or four layers make a substantial trim. Keep overlapping and fusing layers with the iron until you've created a very long skinny piece. Measure and mark a piece 1 1/2 x 100 inches (3.8 x 254 cm) long. Alternatively, you can make two 50-inch (127 cm) long pieces and overlap the ends as you sew them onto the bag in step 13.

5 & 6 Turn the main piece facedown and measure 12 inches (30.5 cm) from the bottom end (opposite of the flap end), and mark a horizontal line. Center the bottom/side piece side-to-side and pin, with its edge lining up with the horizontal line. Sew along the perimeter of where the bottom and the main piece overlap, as shown in the diagram at left. This will be the double-layered bottom to your messenger bag.

7 Again, refer to the diagram at left. Fold the front edge and the side pieces up so they meet to make the corner, and pin together, with the seam to the outside. Next bring the back up to make the back corner and pin. Continue working your way up the side, pinning the front to the side and the back to the side. All this is done with wrong-sides together. For this project, the seams are on the outside.

8 Start at the top edge where the side meets the back, and sew a 1/4 inch (0.6 cm) seam down the side, across the bottom, and up the other side where the front and side meet. This creates the side of your bag. Repeat on the other side.
(continued on page 36)

9

10

11

12

9 Cut about 1/2 inch (1.3 cm) off both edges of the top tab of the side pieces as shown.

10 On each side of the front flap, use a plate or other circle template to mark a pleasing rounded corner. Cut along the marked line.

11 & 12 Starting where the front meets the side, center the trim over the seam edge and begin folding and pinning it in place. When you reach a corner, fold and tuck in a triangle of trim to make a square corner, much as you'd do if wrapping a present. Check that the corner looks good from either side, then continue around the corner, and up the other side. Continue to pin the trim into position, easing it around the front flap's rounded corners until all seams are trimmed. You can splice the trim together in some inconspicuous place along the way by overlapping the two pieces of fold-over trim 1/2 inch (1.3 cm) or so.

13

14

15

16

13 Topstitch along the trim's inside edge. (See Topstitching on page 14.) Be sure to remove pins before you sew over them, flattening the bag down as you sew around the bottom corners.

17

18

19

20

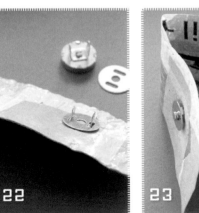

21

22

23

24

14 & 15 Thread the tab on the side through the bottom rung of your buckle slide, and pin. Sew it into place with two rows of stitching about $1/4$ inch (0.6 cm) from the slide's bottom. Repeat on other side.

16–21 Next, thread about 2 inches (5.1 cm) of one strap end around the middle rung of the third buckle slide. Sew the end down with two lines of stitching (photo 16). Then thread the other raw end through the buckle slide on the bag's left side with the wrong side of the strap facing out (photo 17). Next, bring the raw end up through the buckle slide attached to the strap's other end, then over the middle rung, and out (photos 18 and 19). Finally, thread the raw end through the slide buckle attached to the bag's right side (photo 20). Fold the strap back on itself about 2 inches (5.1 cm), and sew into place (photo 21).

22 You'll need to attach both male and female pieces of the magnetic closure to tabs so the back hardware doesn't show. The female tab goes on the bag; the male, on the flap. First cut a piece of scrap fused-plastic $2 1/2$ x 6 inches (6.4 x 15.2 cm) for the male tab and $1 3/4$ x $3 1/2$ inches (4.4 x 8.9 cm) for the female. Mark a point on the male tab so that it's centered $1 1/4$ inch (3.2 cm) from both the tab's bottom and sides. Push the prongs of the magnetic piece through the mark, and slide the metal reinforcement piece over the prongs. Bend the prongs down to the outside over the metal reinforcement to secure. Repeat with the female tab, centering the closure so it's $7/8$ inch (2.2 cm) from both the tab's bottom and sides.

23 & 24 Fold the tab in half with the right sides out, and topstitch around the perimeter.

25 & 26 Attach the female tab to the center bottom of the front of the bag and the male tab to the flap's center. Sew in place. Note: Sewing the female tab on the bag requires a little squashing and squeezing of the fabric at this point to get the machine needle into position. Although it'd be easier to sew this in place when the bag material is still flat, you'd have to guess where to place it. Waiting until the bag is almost done allows you to tweak the placement of the closure so it works perfectly.

27 You can leave the tab plain or add a button or other decorative element. I raided the hardware aisle for this cool metal washer, then found a bright button to go with it. Because the button is larger than the hole in the washer, once you sew the button on (going through the hole in the washer), it holds the washer in place.

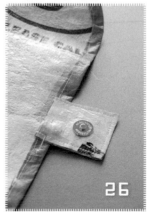

25 26 27

EASE LEVEL:	rank beginners & beyond
TIME REQUIREMENT:	less than an hour
COST:	might be nothing at all
ECO BROWNIE POINTS:	a whole sackful

T-Shirt MARKET BAG

Sew a tote, save a tree. This shopping tote takes less than an hour to make from start to finish. Recycle a couple old T-shirts to make this a double-layer, double-strength tote that is cool to carry and easy to craft. Of course, the shirts work just as well if they're completely plain, but let your inner artist loose and add a little abstract embellishment.

Materials & Tools

- basic tool kit (see page 9)

FOR THE LIGHT BLUE BAG:

- 2 large cotton T-shirts

FOR THE GREEN BAG:

- 3 large cotton T-shirts
- scrap of T-shirt material in 4th color (optional)

Sew first, then cut

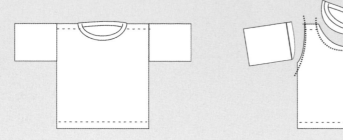

First sew the two T-shirts together at the shoulders and across the bottom hem. Then cut away the sleeves and the neckline to make a useful tote.

Here's how

1 & 2 Choose two T-shirts in fun, snazzy colors. Put one inside the other, wrong sides together, with the shirt that will be the tote's lining color on the outside. Pin and connect the two shirts by stitching along the old shoulder seams. Then pin and sew the two shirts together along the bottom hem. The T-shirt already has side seams.

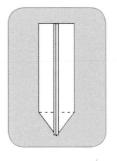

3 Make this simple gusset: Smooth open one side so the side seam is flat and centered, and comes to a point. Measure about 2 inches (5.1 cm) up from the point, and sew horizontally across the side seam as shown. Repeat on the other side.

4 Turn the bag so the main color is on the outside. You should have a nice square gusset with the original side seam centered as shown here.

5 Cut off the arms of the shirts a little to the inside of original seam. Cut out the neck of the old shirts, creating a nice curve that dips down about 6 inches (15.2 cm) or so. These will be your new tote's handles.

6 Pin the inner and outer shirts to one another at both the armholes and at the neck. Sew them together about 1/2 inch from the edge, using a fat zigzag stitch or overcast stitch.

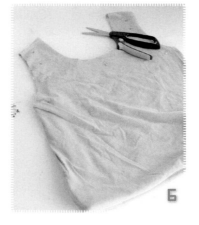

Add some attitude

Using a fat zigzag or a serger-style over-cast stitch, sew a cluster of circles, ovals, rounded squares, etc., to your liking onto the T-shirt tote.

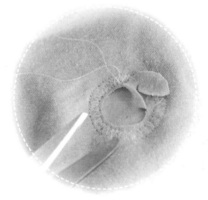

With extra-sharp scissors, use tiny snips to cut out the interior of the circle. Cut through just one layer of fabric to expose the lining fabric beneath.

Okay, full disclosure: This green tote is actually a three-T-tote. It's lime green, purple, and then teal on the inside. I wanted to experiment with a heftier bag that held its shape nicely even when carrying all my weightiest possessions. The bonus was I could expose three different colors in the cut-away reverse appliqué process. But was that enough for me? Apparently not. To add a little shot of sunshine yellow, I first made a small hole through the first two layers of the bag (leaving the teal layer intact.) Then I stuffed a little rectangle of yellow through the hole and smoothed it out. Finally, I sewed around the outside of the yellow rectangle and cut a little peek-a-boo hole out of the purple layer to expose the yellow beneath.

wear it!

Fuzzy Slipper Boots

Furry Trapper's Hat

Buttoned-Up Baubles • Quick, Cute, Clever Jacket • Piece-ful Easy Scarf • Nip & Tuck T-Shirt

EASE LEVEL: *audacity more useful than skill*

TIME REQUIREMENT: *about the time it takes bread to rise*

COST: *flannel is cheap*

HIPNESS FACTOR: *the ultimate in slacker-chic*

Fuzzy SLIPPER BOOTS

These boots are handmade for those lazy days when you stay in your pajamas and let someone else cook the pancakes for a change. Your washing machine is the power tool here, transforming mundane flannel into magic slippers. Your toes, trapped all day in your more sensible shoes, will long for this fluffy, home-made chenille. Make two pairs and keep one under your desk? Hmmm...now that sounds sensible to me.

Materials & Tools

- basic tool kit (see page 9)

- pattern pieces from pages 124-125

- 3/4 yard (68.6 cm) of cotton flannel for the boot's outside

- 2 yards (1.8 m) of contrasting cotton flannel for the three-layer lining (preshrink all flannel before using!)

- 2 square feet (61 cm) or about 1/3 yard (30.5 cm) of washable leather, suede, vinyl, or heavy felt for the sole
    OR
- 2 pre-made slipper soles (available at some fabric stores or online)

- washing machine/dryer

- stiff bristled brush (optional)

Make the cut

Before cutting, be sure to preshrink all the flannel fabric in a washing machine filled with hot water and a hot dryer. Also make sure that the material you use for the outer sole is washable.

lining fabric—cut 6 of each piece (see pages 124-125 for pattern pieces)

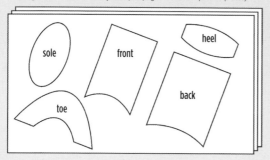

outer sole—cut 2

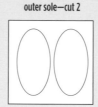

outer fabric—cut 2 of each piece

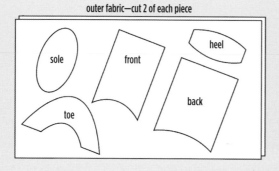

It'd be very difficult, and probably a bit depressing, to try to cut through six layers of fabric when cutting out the many layers of lining fabric necessary for this project. It's probably best to cut them two layers at a time and consider it your meditation in patience for the day.

Cut the flannel pieces on the bias, or diagonal, of the fabric. This ensures that there are very few seams that are perfectly tangent to the grain of the fabric and you'll get better "frays." This doesn't need to be "true" bias—45 degrees to the straight grain of the fabric. Just put everything at a jaunty angle, and you should be fine.

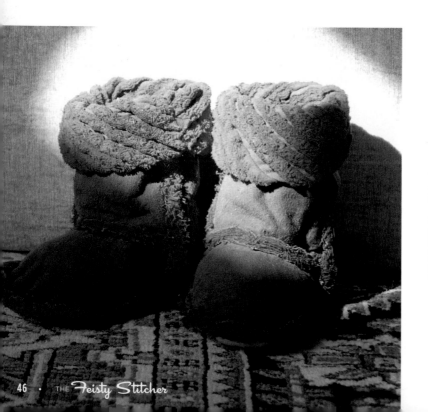

Since these boots are so soft and squishy, it isn't necessary to make them specifically for the right or left foot. The fit is pretty easy and unstructured and feels more like a sock than a shoe. The sizing on the pattern is approximate and based on foot length rather than shoe size. See the pattern pieces on pages 124-125 for specifics.

Here's how

1 Cut out the various pieces for the boots, as per the cutting instructions at left. (See pattern pieces on pages 124-125.)

2 For each boot piece, layer together the three lining pieces and one outer fabric piece. Pin them together.

3 Sew the four layers of each piece together, stitching around the perimeter 1/2 inch (1.3 cm) in from the edge.

4 & 5 To make the fuzzy cuff on the boots, use the ruler to measure 6 inches (15.2 cm) from the straight top end of one of the front pieces. Define the cuff area by marking and sewing a horizontal line. Next, mark and then sew a diagonal line from the top corner to the bottom corner of this cuff area. Now mark and sew parallel lines at 1/2-inch (1.3 cm) intervals across the entire cuff area, as shown. Repeat on the other front piece and the two back pieces.

6 Using nice sharp scissors, carefully cut between the parallel lines of stitching on the lining sides of the front and back boot pieces. Cut down through the three layers of red lining, being very sure you don't cut through (or even nick) the brown outer layer, as this is what holds the pieces together. It can be a little tedious to start the cut, but if you make a tiny snip with the very tips of the scissors, you should be able to get the scissor blade in and get going. It's easier if you make two passes, cutting through two layers at a time.

(continued on page 48)

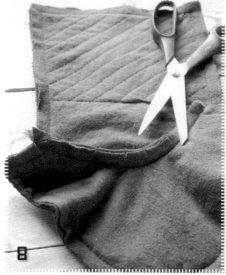

Here's how
(continued)

7 The raw seams are on the outside, so put all pieces together with the wrong sides facing. Start by matching the curved bottom edge of the front piece to the curved arch of the toe piece. Then attach the curved edge of the heel piece to the curved edge of the back piece. Pin and sew together along the stitching from step 3.

8 Clip the seams along the curves. This will help the fabric get a better fray.

9 Attach the front of the boot to the back along the side seams. Pin, then sew. You'll be sewing over many layers of fabric at the intersection of seams, so just take it nice and slow, and be sure to remove any pins before sewing over them.

10 Sew the outer sole to the fabric sole.

11 & 12 Attach the sole to the upper boot, matching center front and center back. Pin first, then sew.

13 Now put your boots into the washing machine/dryer for some hot suds, then a long tumble. Once dry, give them a little "haircut" to even up the fray, and cut off any long threads.

It's great to launder your boots with something rough like jeans to help bring up the fabric's "bloom." Don't wash them with anything linty, like towels, or you'll be picking off fuzz forever more. The ones pictured needed only one wash to come out looking like this. If you want more fuzziness quickly without laundering, use a stiff-bristled brush to bring up even more fray.

EASE LEVEL:	intermediate
TIME REQUIREMENT:	surprisingly fast for such high fashion
COST:	not much fabric here
UNUSUAL TOOLS:	vacuum for flyaway fur

Furry TRAPPER'S HAT

This hat used to be curtains in a circa 1950s hotel. Perhaps I was inspired by multiple viewings of *The Sound of Music* (remember when Maria makes all the Von Trapp children's clothing out of curtains?), but I couldn't rest until these became something wearable and adorable. The faux fur was a necessity, of course. But so are the ties since people threaten to steal it right off my head whenever I wear mine!

Materials & Tools

- basic tool kit (see page 9)
- pattern pieces on page 126
- 1/2 yard (45.7 cm) of barkcloth or similar fabric
- 1/2 yard (45.7 cm) of good quality faux fur
- vacuum or damp cloth
- cotton webbing for straps

Faux fur is ridiculously easy to sew. The needle cuts through even the thick stuff like butter. However, cutting fur is a messy business, making for a lot of tickle-y, sneezy, fuzzy things floating around. Have a vacuum handy to keep the fur from flying. A dampened cloth also works well to pick up the tufts. Remember to take each cut piece outside and shake it off before sewing. This simple step makes faux fur as easy and fun to work with as it is to wear.

Make the cut

Use pattern pieces on page 126, except for the hatband, which is a simple rectangle with the dimensions shown here.

Cut one each of all pieces in outer barkcloth and inner fur.

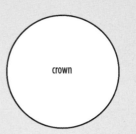

crown

25, 26.5" (63.5, 67.3 cm)

hatband

4 1/2" (11.4 cm)

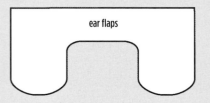

ear flaps

visor

Putting it together

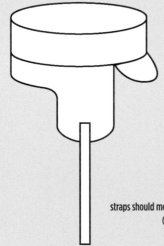

straps should measure a minimum of 22" (55.9 cm)

1

2

3

4

5

6

Here's how

1 & 2 Use the extra-sharp scissors to cut the fabric and the faux-fur lining, as per the cutting instructions at left. See the pattern on page 126. (Hint: If you cut the barkcloth pieces first, they make easy pattern pieces for cutting the fur.) Be sure to vacuum or wipe up all the excess fur pile often.

3 Pin the barkcloth and the fur earflap pieces together, right sides facing. Machine-sew around the perimeter (1/2 inch [1.3 cm] seam), leaving the top edge open. Clip the curves carefully to minimize bulky seams. Repeat with the visor piece. Turn both pieces right side out, and baste across the top edges to hold them in place.

4 With right sides facing, sew the hatband ends together to make a ring. Now you'll attach the earflaps and the visor to the bottom of the hatband. center the earflap piece on either side of the seam in the hatband, and then pin and sew with right sides together. Stitch all the way around the hatband to secure. All seams are 1/2 inch (1.3 cm).

5 Again, with right sides together, pin and sew the crown to the top edge of the hatband 1/2 inch from the edge.

6 Pin the fur crown to the fur hatband, right sides facing. Sew in place, being careful to remove the pins before you sew over them.

(continued on page 54)

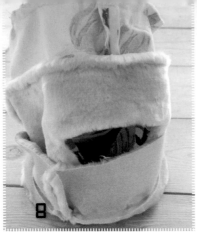

7 Take a minute to trim the seams on the fur crown to keep the bulk down. Lay the crown down on a table with the fur side in.

8 Now place the other piece of the hat (the one with the barkcloth crown, earflaps, and visor) inside the fur crown. The barkcloth piece should be wrong-side out, as shown.

9 Stuff the barkcloth piece all the way down inside the fur crown until the two hatbands are fur-to-fur. Pin the two pieces together at the edge of the hatbands as shown. Sew 1/2-inch [1.3 cm] seam, making sure to leave a 3-inch (7.6 cm) gap for turning.

10 Turn the hat right side out through the gap, then hand sew the hole closed.

11 Attach the ties to the earflaps with a simple box stitch. Finish the end with a tight zigzag.

There are lots of vintage barkcloth pieces waiting for a little modern chutzpah to give them new life. Check at junk or thrift stores, or search the word barkcloth at one of the online auction sites. A recent search of mine turned up tropical florals, atomic age-inspired abstracts from the early 1960s, as well as circus prints and lots of cowboys.

Buttoned-Up BAUBLES

Materials & Tools

- basic tool kit (see page 9)

- scraps of wool, wool-blend or eco-felt* in your choice of colors

- heavyweight thread in black and white

- 1 1/2-inch (3.8 cm) covered button forms

- pencil with eraser

- spool of thread (for pressing the back of the button)

  Eco-felt is felt made from recycled plastic water bottles. It is dense and cushy, and feels more like natural fiber felt than like flimsy acrylic craft felt. It is available in a rainbow of colors at most big-box fabric stores.

Who's got the button? Can't find the perfect button for your project? Make it yourself. These are made with scraps of felt that are layered and sewn for lots of color and character. Cover-your-own-button blanks come in lots of sizes. Learn the technique in just a few minutes, and you'll have a limitless source of custom buttons.

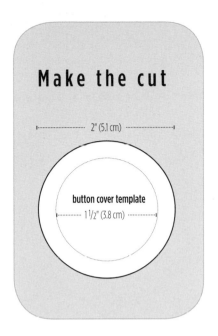

Make the cut

|------ 2" (5.1 cm) ------|

button cover template
1¹/₂" (3.8 cm)

Here's how

1 Cut a 2-inch (5.1 cm) felt circle. Machine-sew a pattern on it, using heavyweight thread. Place the button form top facedown on the fabric's wrong side.

2, 3 & 4 Pull the felt around to the back of the button form, hooking the fabric on the metal teeth. Work your way around the form, pulling the fabric tight as you go. Use the pencil eraser to push the fabric onto the metal teeth. The fabric should hook snugly on the teeth, with the excess pushed down into the hollow of the inside of the button form.

5 Place the button back over the fabric covered form, centering the wire loop through the center hole in the button back.

6 Use the large spool of thread to help push the button back down into position. Press firmly on the spool until you feel the back pop into place. Check that the back is on firmly and is holding the button fabric in place so the fabric is taut.

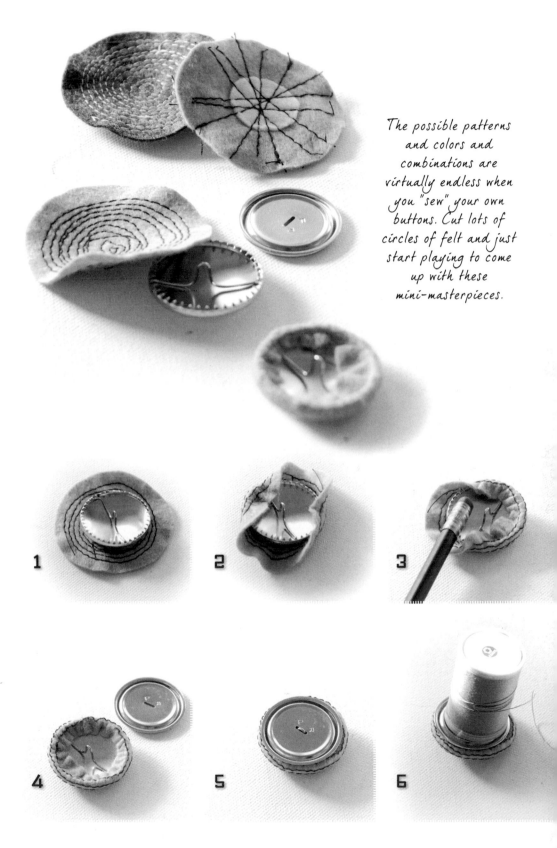

The possible patterns and colors and combinations are virtually endless when you "sew" your own buttons. Cut lots of circles of felt and just start playing to come up with these mini-masterpieces.

These sewn buttons derive all their character from the bold graphic patterns sewn on their surfaces.

Sewn Jewelry

You can turn your favorite sewn buttons into a bracelet or necklace. Simply string them onto a piece of cord or elastic that's cut to size. Make them in colors to match your favorite duds, or just let the sewn designs speak for themselves.

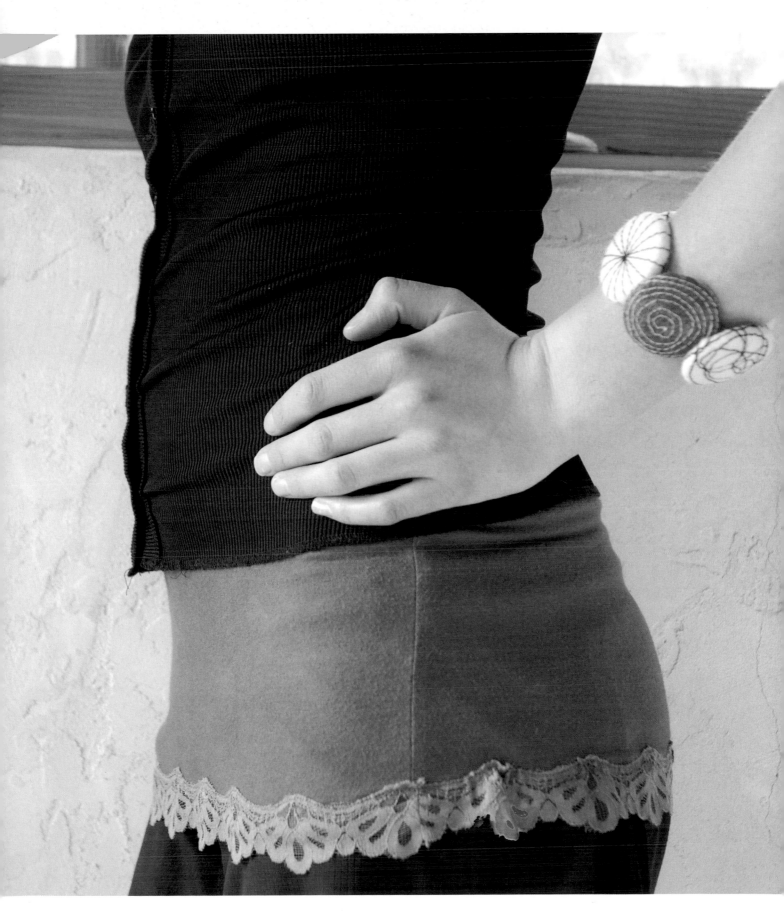

EASE LEVEL: *this one's a breeze*

TIME REQUIREMENT: *basic jacket =* **45** *minutes*
add **15** *minutes each for*
☐ *hood*
☐ *contrasting cuffs*
☐ *the linen version*

COST: *moderate*

USEFULNESS FACTOR: *might just replace the blazer*

Quick, Cute, Clever JACKET

Nothing but rectangles. If you can cut a straight line and sew a straight stitch, you can make this jacket. This super easy pattern, adapted from the historic Japanese kimono, requires no template and no set-in sleeves or complicated collars. Once you buy the fabric, you can have a jacket ready-to-wear in one hour! It's that simple, that smart, and infinitely adaptable. You can add a hood or pockets, contrasting cuffs, make it shorter or longer, wider or narrower. It's so easy and so much fun, you won't be able to stop at just one.

Materials & Tools

- basic tool kit (see page 9)

- 2 yards (1.8 m) of fleece
  (cotton or cotton/poly blend) in heather gray

- 1/2 yard (45.7 cm) of cotton knit or fleece in olive green (lining for the optional hood)

- white thread

Make the cut
(kimono version)

Be sure to preshrink all the fabrics beforehand. To make the simplest, quickest version of this jacket, use no-fray fabrics like cotton or polyester fleece, boiled wool, wool melton, or bouclé. These fabrics don't even require a hem—just a couple of rows of stitching to give the edge some finish. The pattern below shows two lengths: one for the shorter jacket shown on page 60 and another for both the longer jacket shown at left and the blue linen one shown on page 65.

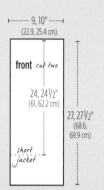

front *cut two*

9, 10"
(22.9, 25.4 cm)

24, 24½"
(61, 62.2 cm)

27, 27½"
(68.6,
69.9 cm)

*short
jacket*

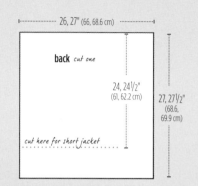

back *cut one*

26, 27" (66, 68.6 cm)

24, 24½"
(61, 62.2 cm)

27, 27½"
(68.6,
69.9 cm)

cut here for short jacket

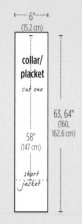

collar/
placket

cut one

6"
(15.2 cm)

63, 64"
(160,
162.6 cm)

58"
(147 cm)

*short
jacket*

sleeves

cut two

23, 23½" (58.4, 59.7 cm)

*To make shaped sleeves, cut
the rectangle as specified,
then fold in half. Measure
in 3 1/2 inches (8.9cm)
from the cut edges and cut
a diagonal line from
this point to the
opposite corner.*

25"
(63.5 cm)

3½"
(8.9 cm)

Traditional kimonos were one-size-fits-all affairs, which worked fine since the fit is simple and loose. This pattern also fits a surprisingly diverse array of body types, but I made the jackets in two sizes: a smallish one that fits small/medium and a biggish one that fits large/extra-large. Both are styled for women. You could certainly scale the patterns up a bit to make a natty little jacket for a guy. On the pattern pieces, the first number is for the smallish jacket, the second for the biggish.

SHOULDER SEAMS

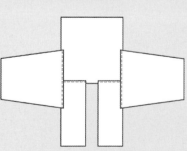

Connect the two
front pieces to the
back along the top
edge to make the
shoulder seams.

ADD SLEEVES

Add the sleeves at
either side, centering
them on the shoulder
seams.

SIDE SEAMS

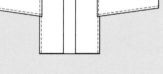

Fold the jacket in half
along the shoulder
seams, and sew the
side and arm seams.

COLLAR PLACKET

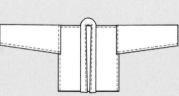

Fold the collar piece,
and attach it across
the neck and down the
fronts of the jacket.

Here's how (kimono version)

1 Cut out the jacket pieces, as specified at left. Sew the front pieces to the back along the top edge, with right sides facing, as shown. Sew one seam 1/2 inch (1.3 cm) from the edge, then sew another line of stitching 1/4 inch (0.6 cm) closer to the edge. Trim excess as shown. (This double seam isn't strictly necessary when using a no-fray fabric, but it makes a very nice, neat, long-lasting seam.) Once you've sewn the two front pieces to the back, open the whole construction out flat and right-side up. Mark the center point on the sleeve's top. Place the sleeve, right sides facing, so the center point lines up with the shoulder seam you've just sewn and the sleeve's top edge. Pin and sew the sleeve into place. Repeat for the other sleeve.

2 & 3 Flip the sleeves over and then fold the construction in half along the shoulder seams, right sides together. Line up the underarm seam and the jacket's side seam. Pin and sew as before. Be sure to press the armhole seams toward the sleeve as shown. Repeat on the other side. If you are going to make the hoodie version of this jacket, skip to step 7 on the following page.

4 Fold the jacket collar/placket in half down the center with wrong sides together. Starting at the center of the back of the jacket, align the raw edges of the collar piece with the raw edge of the neck of the jacket, and pin. Work down both sides of the jacket front, pinning the collar/placket along the front edge.

5 Sew the seam 1/2 inch (1.3 cm) from the edge. This seam will be a bit bulky since it's three layers of fabric. To reduce the bulk, open up the seam and trim the center piece of excess fabric close to the stitching. Sew a second line of stitching and then trim the excess, as in step 1.

6 For the hem on both the sleeves and the jacket bottom, you can simply do a double row of topstitching to stabilize and "finish" the hem. (See Topstitching on page 14.) Sew a row 1/2 inch (1.3 cm) from the bottom, then move up 1/4 inch (0.6 cm) and repeat. Trim close to the stitching as shown. You're done!

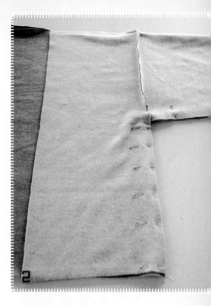

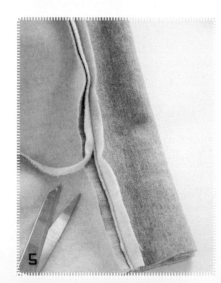

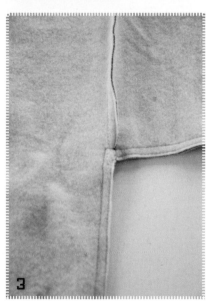

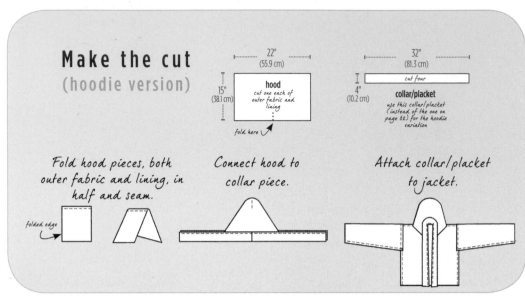

Make the cut
(hoodie version)

22"
(55.9 cm)

15"
(38.1 cm)

hood
cut one each of
outer fabric and
lining

fold here

32"
(81.3 cm)

4"
(10.2 cm)

cut four

collar/placket
use this collar/placket
(instead of the one on
page 62) for the hoodie
variation

Fold hood pieces, both
outer fabric and lining, in
half and seam.

folded edge

Connect hood to
collar piece.

Attach collar/placket
to jacket.

8

Here's how (hoodie version)

7 Fold each hood rectangle in half, right sides together, so it measures 15 x 11 inches (38.1 x 27.9 cm). Sew along the top edge.

8 Unfold both hood rectangles. Put the hood and the lining together with right sides facing. Sew around all raw edges, leaving a 3-inch (7.6 cm) gap so you can turn the hood right-side out.

9 Turn the hood right side out through the gap. Note that the seam will be at the back of the hood in the finished jacket. Sew two collar pieces together, using a 1/2- inch (1.3 cm) seam, to make a long strip 63 x4 inches (160 x 10.2 cm). Repeat with the other collar pieces to create two long strips for the collar/placket.

10 Line up the hood seam with the center of the collar pieces. Sandwich the hood in between the two collar pieces with the right sides toward the hood. Line up the edges, pin and sew. Trim the seams to make them less bulky, then open the seams so the right sides of the collars are facing out.

11 Pin the raw edges of the collar piece to the raw edge of the jacket neck and front right sides together. Be sure to line up the center of the collar piece with the center back of the jacket. Sew with a seam as shown in step 5, and finish the jacket as in step 6.

TRY IT IN LINEN. This jacket, made from two colors of luscious linen, uses the same pattern and techniques as the one shown on the preceding pages, with one notable difference. Because linen is a fabric that frays, it was necessary to finish the interior seams. I used French seams for this jacket (see French Seam on page 11). I also hemmed the jacket bottom and made contrasting cuffs. Please add $^1/_4$ inch (0.6 cm) to each side of all the pattern pieces to allow for the deeper seams. Follow the directions on the preceding pages, substituting French seams for all flat seams.

TO MAKE THE CONTRASTING CUFFS, use the cut jacket sleeves from step 1 as your pattern. Cut two pieces of contrasting fabric to be the same width as your jacket sleeves but only about one-half their height. Fold the cuffs down the center and sew them together with a French seam, (this is the underarm seam for the cuff). Fold the top edge of the cuff down $^1/_4$ inch (0.6 cm), then fold again and sew to make a $^1/_2$ inch (1.3 cm) hem. Attach the bottom/raw edge of the cuff to the bottom of the jacket sleeve (right sides together) aligning the underarm seams of the sleeve and the cuff. Sew a $^1/_2$-inch (1.3 cm) seam. Turn the cuff up into the interior of the sleeve and machine or hand stitch into place.

EASE LEVEL: *embarrassingly easy*

TIME REQUIREMENT: *could make a dozen-a-day*

COST: *depends on access to old sweaters*

UNUSUAL TOOLS: *machine with an overcast stitch*

Piece-ful EASY SCARF

Up to your neck in old sweaters? Have you ever accidentally washed your favorite wool sweater in really hot water and had it come out looking like a tea cozy? Although a sad day for your sweater, it's just that transformation that makes this scrumptiously soft scarf possible. Fun to mix and match, simple to stitch together, it's a great way to make a warm and fuzzy scarf without ever touching a knitting needle.

Materials & Tools

- basic tool kit (see page 9)

- about six 100 percent wool sweaters (*not* machine washable sweaters); in addition to sheep's wool, also consider cashmere, alpaca, and angora

- washing machine/dryer

- small piece of stiff cardboard

- pen

- craft scissors

- contrasting thread

- iron (optional)

Make the cut This will make a scarf that is 9 x 75 inches (22.9 x 190.5 cm).

3 1/2"
(8.9 cm)

8"
(20.3 cm)

individual
sweater piece
or "brick"
cut 28

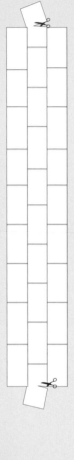

You can make the scarf wider (by adding entire columns) or longer by adding pieces top and bottom. Or you could enlarge the scarf by making the individual "bricks" a little wider or taller.

To "felt" the sweaters

Start with 100 percent wool fiber sweaters (sheep's wool, cashmere, angora, or alpaca) in a variety of colors and patterns. Machine-wash them in hot water, and tumble dry in a hot dryer. This will shrink and tangle the fibers to make a dense, fray-free felted fabric that's warm, fuzzy, and easy to work with. Repeat if necessary to get a satisfying level of felting.

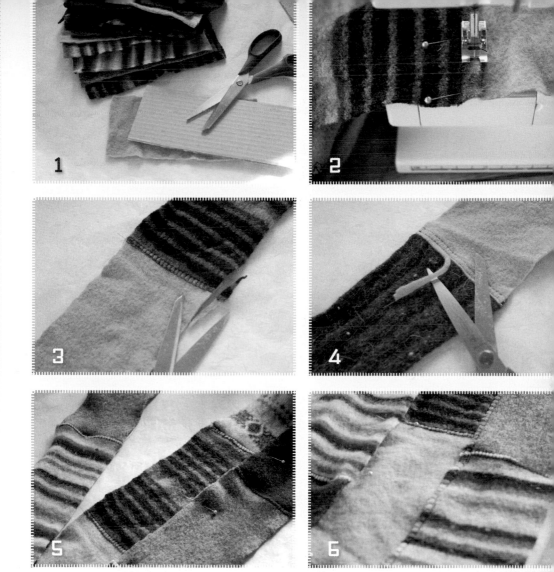

Here's how

1 Use the craft scissors to cut out a 3½ x 8-inch (8.9 x 20.3 cm) cardboard rectangle. Use this cardboard template to cut 28 "bricks" out of the felted sweaters.

2 Set your machine to an overcast stitch (a wide zigzag works too). Experiment with a fabric scrap until you get the width you want. Pin together two bricks along the short end, overlapping each piece about ¼ inch (0.6 cm). Sew together with the overcast stitch.

3 & 4 Make the side edges straight by snipping off any "bulge" created by the seam. Then trim the seam so it's flush to the stitching on both sides of the scarf. Repeat steps 2, 3, and 4 to make two nine-brick-long columns and one 10-brick-long column.

5 Pin the 10-brick column to one nine-brick column on the long side. Let the seams offset by about half a brick, top to bottom, to make a more interesting pattern. Overlap the two columns about ¼ inch (0.6 cm) and pin, sew, and trim just as before.

6 Add the third column (the other nine-brick one) on the other side of the 10-brick column. Pin, sew, and trim as before. Cut the excess length off of the 10-brick column to even up the scarf's top and bottom. You can use a warm iron to "block" the scarf, (in other words, flatten and square it up). Trim any uneven edges or errant threads to finish.

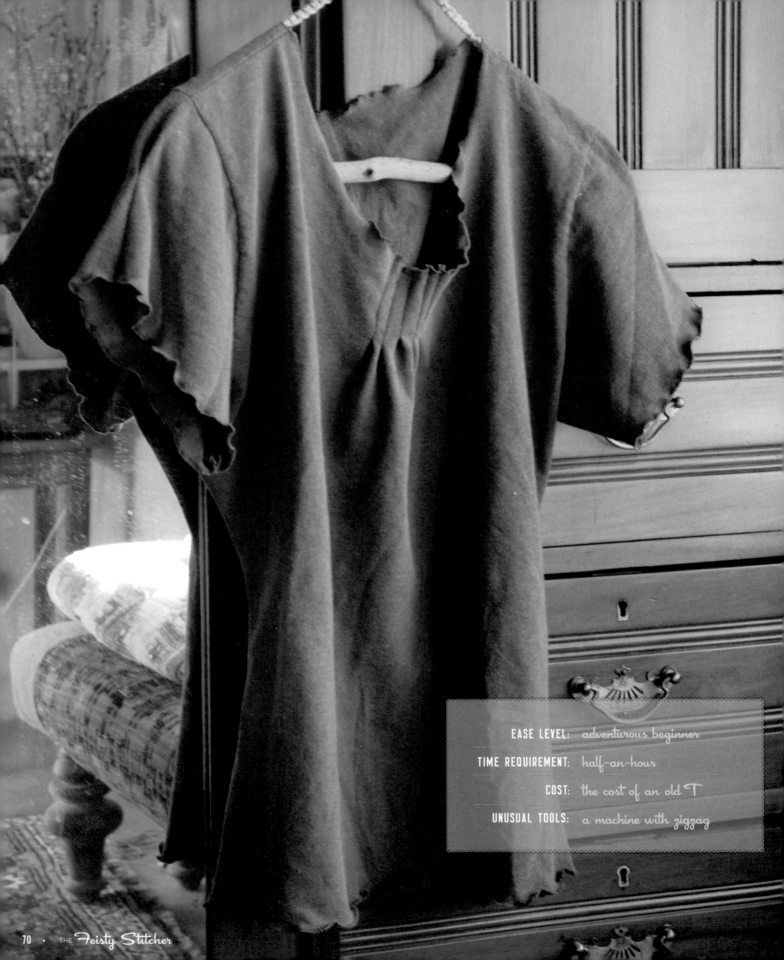

EASE LEVEL: adventurous beginner

TIME REQUIREMENT: half-an-hour

COST: the cost of an old T

UNUSUAL TOOLS: a machine with zigzag

Nip & Tuck T-SHIRT

Tailored to a T! Darts and tailoring and alterations always seem a bit scary—a mysterious science better left to designers in ateliers or seamstresses in back rooms. But a men's recycled T-shirt offers the perfect opportunity to play with fitting something to your body. Use a couple of well-placed seams, a little nip here, a little tuck there to make a prosaic old shirt feminine, quirky, and flattering.

Materials & Tools

- basic tool kit (see page 9)
- men's recycled T-shirt size XL
- tape measure
- salad plate or circle template

Make the cut

I started with a men's XL to make a shirt that fits my women's medium-sized frame. The beauty of this project is that you can keep playing with the fit by sewing more or fewer tucks at the top and nipping the side and back seams in more or less. It's a quirky experiment that doesn't worry about perfection.

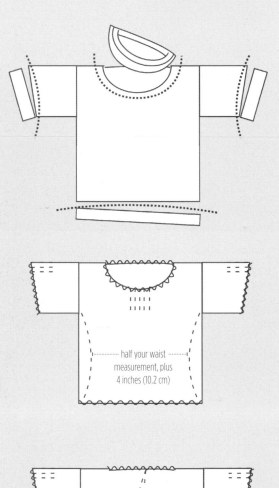

half your waist measurement, plus 4 inches (10.2 cm)

the center back seam allows you to adjust the fit even further

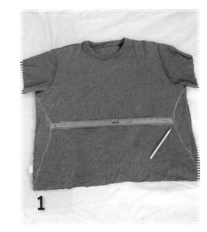

1

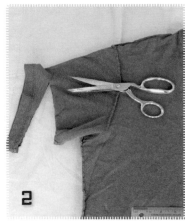

2

3

4

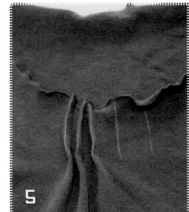

5

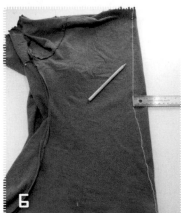

6

Here's how

1 Measure your waist. Halve the number, then add 4 inches (10.2 cm) to get the working measurement. Turn the shirt inside out, then find the center. Starting from the center, mark a spot on each edge that's equal to one-half your working measurement. Next, freehand draw a curve from the underarm seam through the marks you've just made down to the hem on each side. (The mark should be at the narrowest part of the curve of the waist as shown.) Sew along the lines on each side, then trim the side seams to about ¹/₂ inch (1.3 cm).

2 Cut off the end of the sleeve, starting about ¹/₂ inch (1.3 cm) from the sleeve's bottom edge to about 1 ¹/₂ inches (3.8 cm) at the top. Also cut off the bottom hem of the shirt.

3 Use the bottom third of a salad plate (or some other 8-inch [20.3 cm] circle) to mark the front neckline of the shirt. Cut along the mark in the front. In the back, simply cut off the old neckband.

4 Use a medium zigzag stitch to finish the neckline, sleeve, and bottom hems. Pull the fabric as you sew to create the ruffled edge. Experiment first with one of the scraps cut off from the T-shirt to see how wide and tight you want the zigzag and how much to pull as you sew.

5 At the center front of the neckline, make a 2-inch-long (5.1 cm) straight line. Mark other lines of the same length at 1 inch (2.5 cm) intervals on either side of the center line until you have five lines altogether. Fold the fabric with these lines at the center and pin. Sew a ¹/₄ inch (0.6 cm) seam on the wrong side of the shirt down the length of the line to make these neat little pintucks.*

6 Try the T-shirt on to determine if you want to add a back seam to make the shirt even more fitted. If you do, turn the shirt inside out again and fold t it down the center back. Measure in an inch or two right at the waist and mark. Draw an arc from the bottom hem of the shirt to the top of the neckline that runs through your mark at the waist. Once you have a pleasing arc, pin and sew. Trim the seam to about ¹/₂ inch (1.3 cm).

* You can repeat the pintucks on the top of the sleeve for a slightly more fitted effect. Start at the top of the sleeve and put in three to five pintucks.

Snap-to-It Storage

Ready-to-Roll Mat

Punched-Up Lampshade · Upholstery Webbing Bulletin Board · Barkcloth & Jute Floor Cushions · & More...

EASE LEVEL:	entry-level DIY
COST:	same as root beer floats for two
UNEXPECTED MATERIALS:	the odd lamp part
STYLE QUOTIENT:	metro retro

Punched-Up LAMPSHADE

Your machine packs a punch. When you "sew" on paper without thread, you can create row upon row of perfect little perforations. These tiny holes let the light stream through, creating a luminous pattern on even the most ordinary paper. I used a simple pattern of undulating waves to make this retro lampshade ultra mod.

Materials & Tools

- basic tool kit (see page 9)

- craft blade

- 2 pieces of mid- to heavy weight paper in your choice of color, each 11 x 17 inches (27.9 x 43.2 cm) (one piece is for the lampshade proper; the other is for the small strips and can be in a contrasting color if you choose)

- paper glue

- matching thead

- 3 small grommets

- grommet setter and hammer

- 3-armed lampshade spider

- paperclips or clothespins

- 3 ball finials for the spider's arms (if it doesn't come with them already)

- light socket with about 8 feet (2.4 m) of electrical cord attached

- tools and instructions for simple wiring

- wire cutters

- electrical plug

NOTE: Use only a compact fluorescent bulb with this lampshade for safety reasons as well as eco-friendly ones. Fluorescents burn more efficiently, giving off much less wasteful heat, which cuts down any fire risk.

Make the cut

17" (43.2 cm)

11" (27.9 cm)

main piece
with strips at top and bottom

1/2" (1.3 cm)

11" (27.9 cm)

Reinforcement strips at the top and bottom are one layer of the same or contrasting paper sewn in place.

To complete this lampshade, you'll need a couple of lamp parts from the hardware store or online lamp parts outlet.

First of all, you'll need a thing called a "spider" for the top of the lamp. They come in 3- and 4-arm varieties. Either works fine. You'll also need ball finials (another common lamp part) for the threaded ends of the spider. They come in a variety of sizes and types. Choose a style that suits your fancy.

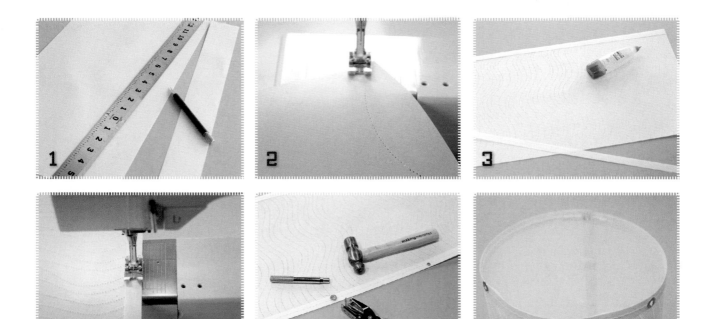

Here's how

1 Use a craft knife and a straightedge to cut out the three paper pieces, as specified at left.

2 Remove all the thread from your machine. Set your machine to a very long straight stitch so the holes in the paper aren't too close together. Begin on the shorter edge of the main piece of paper, and sew an undulating line of stitching from top to bottom. Stitch a second line of stitching parallel to, and about 1/2 inch (1.3 cm) over from, the first line. Continue until you've covered the entire surface with parallel curvy lines.

3 & 4 Position the thin paper strips at the top and bottom edges of the stitched paper. Use a few tiny dots of glue to "pin" them in place. Thread your machine to match the color of the paper strips. Machine sew a straight stitch down the middle to secure the strips.

5 You'll need three grommet holes for your three-armed spider. It'll generally be easier to set the first two grommets before you glue the flat paper into a cylinder. (The third will sit right on the seam and go through all layers of paper.) Measure in 1/4 inch (0.6 cm) from one side edge of the lampshade's top side and mark. Repeat on the other side. Now measure the distance between those marks, and divide by three; for example, for an 11 x 17-inch (27.9 x 43.2 cm) lampshade, the overall distance will be 16 1/2 inches (41.9 cm) so the distance between the holes will be 5 1/2 inches (14 cm). Install the grommets at the two marked points in the middle of the paper (not the marks close to the side edge) as per the manufacturer's instructions.

6 Swipe the short edges of the paper with a strong paper glue. Form the flat paper into a cylinder, overlapping the glued edges about

1/2 inch (1.3 cm). Secure top and bottom with the paper clip or clothespin, and allow the glue to set. Tack the top and bottom edges of the cylinder together with a short row of stitching that follows along the stitching from step 4. Add the last grommet hole on this overlapping seam.

To Finish Unscrew the arm-end finials on the spider, then put the spider in place at the top of your lampshade. Next, screw the ball finials back on to hold the spider and the shade in place. To electrify your shade, you'll need basic wiring skills. (If you don't know how, ask your favorite electrician or handyperson). Cut the electrical plug off the socket light fixture so you can thread the cut end of the cord through the spider's center hole. Then reattach the plug to the opposite end, hang it, and light it up!

EASE LEVEL: mid-level manages it

TIME REQUIREMENT: start after breakfast, finish by lunch

UNEXPECTED MATERIALS: upholstery tape

COST: a pittance per yard

Barkcloth & Jute
FLOOR CUSHIONS

In the back, down low on a shelf in just about any big-box fabric store, you'll find a big fat roll of jute upholstery webbing. It costs almost nothing and has a cool vibe that's both homespun and industrial at the same time. Pair it up with some 1950s barkcloth or an outdoor stripe, and you've got vintage with a modern edge.

Materials & Tools

- basic tool kit (see page 9)

- 1¹⁄₂ yards (1.4 m) of barkcloth, canvas, or cotton duck per cushion

- about 10 yards (9.1 m) of jute upholstery webbing for cushion A (see next page)

- angle tool or 3-inch (7.6 cm) square piece of paper to use as template

- matching thread

- 22 x 22 x 3-inch (55.9 x 55.9 x 7.6 cm) box-edge foam pillow insert

Make the cut

This project shows two types of floor cushions: cushion A has a front face that has a fabric inset framed with jute upholstery webbing. Cushion B has a plain fabric front. Both cushions A and B have jute webbing sides, but on cushion A, the seams are on the outside (exposed), while on cushion B, they're on the inside. To keep the exposed seams on cushion A from being raw and frayed, each fabric piece is doubled, sewn, and turned to finish the edges before seaming together in the cushion.

CUSHION A

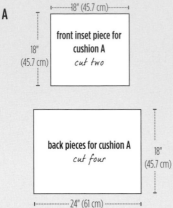

18" (45.7 cm)

18" (45.7 cm)

front inset piece for cushion A
cut two

back pieces for cushion A
cut four

18" (45.7 cm)

24" (61 cm)

CUSHION B

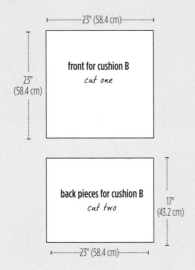

23" (58.4 cm)

23" (58.4 cm)

front for cushion B
cut one

back pieces for cushion B
cut two

17" (43.2 cm)

23" (58.4 cm)

Put it together

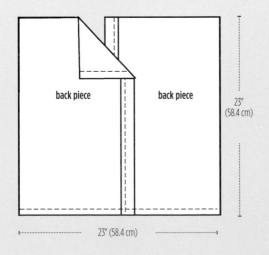

back piece   back piece

23" (58.4 cm)

23" (58.4 cm)

Here's how

To Start Use the scissors and the straightedge to cut out all the necessary pieces of the fabric as per cutting instructions at left. If you're making cushion B, please skip ahead to step 8.

1 Cut four pieces of upholstery webbing, each piece 24 inches (61 cm) long. Put two pieces together, lining up the ends. Starting at the corner, draw a 45° angle across the webbing. You can use an angle tool for this or just cut a 3-inch (7.6 cm) square piece of paper and fold on the diagonal for your pattern. Sew along this diagonal line.

2 Fold open the seam, and pin back the excess fabric.

3 & 4 Machine-sew two lines of topstitching along the seam, one about $1/8$ inch (0.3 cm) in from the seam and the next about $3/8$ inch (0.95 cm). (See Topstitching on page 14.) Trim the excess seam fabric away.

Repeat on the remaining three corners to make the jute "frame."

5 With right sides facing, pin together the two pieces for the front inset piece. Sew a 1/2-inch (1.3 cm) seam around the perimeter, leaving open a 3-inch (7.6 cm) gap for the turn. Clip the corners, turn the fabric, and machine-sew the gap closed.

6 Position the inset in the jute frame, and pin.

7 Topstitch the inset fabric in place within the jute frame by sewing about $1/8$ inch (0.3 cm) from the frame's inside edge, as shown. Trim the fabric to about $1/8$ inch (0.3 cm) from the stitching.

8 Make the overlapping pieces for the cushion back:
FOR CUSHION B, make a narrow hem on one of the rectangle's long edges by folding down the raw

edge 1/2 inch (1.3 cm), then folding that over again another 1/2 inch (1.3 cm). Pin, then sew with a line of stitching close to the folded edge. Repeat to create another identical piece.
FOR CUSHION A, put two of the back fabric pieces together, right sides facing. Pin and sew a 1/2-inch (1.3 cm) seam around the perimeter, leaving open a 3-inch (7.6 cm) gap for the turn. Clip the corners, turn the fabric, and hand sew the gap closed. Fold down the long edge about 1 inch (2.5 cm), pin, and sew in place. Repeat to create another identical piece.
FOR BOTH CUSHIONS A AND B, overlap the two finished pieces by a few inches to make a 23 inches (58.4 cm) square (see diagram on page 82). Stitch down the sides to hold the overlap in place and make it one piece for the back.

(continued on page 85)

Here's how
(continued)

9 To make the sides, cut a 98-inch (2.5 m) length of upholstery webbing. Seam together the two ends to make a giant circle of jute.

10 For cushion A, you will attach the webbing to the front, wrong sides together. For cushion B, it will be right sides together so the seams are on the inside in the finished product. Start with the seam of the webbing circle in the middle of one of the sides of the pillow front. Line up the edges of the webbing and the pillow front and pin together, working toward the corner.

11 It's easiest to pin and sew each side of the pillow individually instead of trying to do the entire perimeter at once. Sew the pinned section together 1/2 inch (1.3 cm) from the edge, stopping the stitching right at the diagonal corner seam on the front piece. This will be your pivot point where you begin working up the next side of the pillow.

12 Make a crease in the side piece right at the corner of the pillow front. Pin the point of the pillow top's corner to the crease in the side.

13 Fold the creased jute side back, and tuck it out of the way. Line up the edges of the webbing and the pillow front, and pin.

14 & 15 Start at the pivot point from step 11. Sew the entire length of the next side, stopping at the corner as before.

16 Continue working sides and corners until you've completed the perimeter and all four corners. Trim the fabric to about 1/8 inch (0.3 cm) from the stitching.

17 Turn the piece over, and position the back of the pillow. Make sure the four corners of the pillow back line up with the four creased corners of the pillow sides. Repeat steps 10 to 16 to pin and sew the back into position. When completed, insert the pillow form through the over-lapping gap in the pillow back.
Note: It's a tight fit, so be prepared for some aerobic activity!

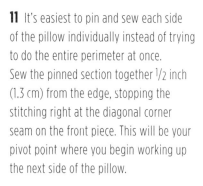

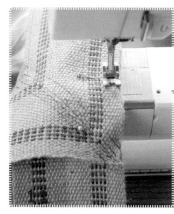

Snap-to-It STORAGE

Oh snap! Got a little too much stuff? These little red stacking bins can hold on to it for you, and do it with lots of impish good style. They come together in a snap—well, eight snaps, to be exact. They're made with a technicolor faux leather laminated with three contrasting awning stripe fabrics. Ready to hold everything from rubberbands to CDs, they're just your size.

Materials & Tools

- basic tool kit (page 9)

- 1^1/$_3$ yards (1.2 m) of faux-leather fabric at least 45 inches (114.3 cm) wide

- 1^1/$_3$ yards (1.2 m) of lining fabric at least 45 inches (114.3 cm) wide

- iron-on adhesive (a.k.a. fusible web)
  This comes in a variety of widths depending on the brand, so you will have to do the math to figure out the amount you will need to cover a surface 1^1/$_3$ yards by 45 inches (1.2 m x 114.3 cm).

- iron

- leather needle for sewing machine (see Specialty Sewing Machine Needles on page 13)

- heavyweight thread

- clothespins

- 24 snaps, ^{1}/$_2$-inch (1.3 cm)

- snap application tool that will work with ^{1}/$_2$-inch snaps (see page 51)

Make the cut

Start by cutting squares of the faux leather, the lining fabric, and the iron-on adhesive. You'll eventually laminate all of them together. These squares should be an inch or two (2.5 to 5.1 cm) larger than the final size you'll need. You may need to piece the adhesive together to get it to cover your entire square. Only after you've laminated the fabric together will you cut out the shapes below.

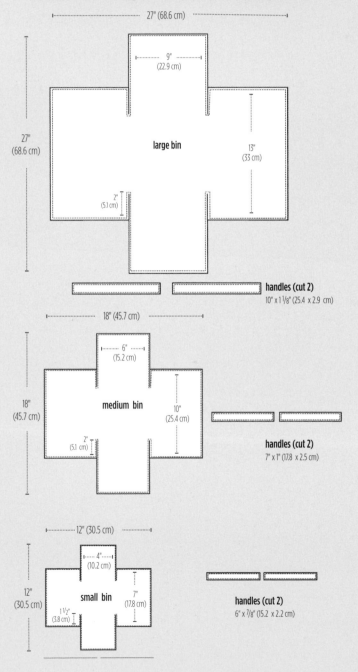

27" (68.6 cm)

9"
(22.9 cm)

large bin

13"
(33 cm)

27"
(68.6 cm)

2"
(5.1 cm)

handles (cut 2)
10" x 1 1/8" (25.4 x 2.9 cm)

18" (45.7 cm)

6"
(15.2 cm)

medium bin

10"
(25.4 cm)

18"
(45.7 cm)

2"
(5.1 cm)

handles (cut 2)
7" x 1" (17.8 x 2.5 cm)

12" (30.5 cm)

4"
(10.2 cm)

small bin

7"
(17.8 cm)

12"
(30.5 cm)

1 1/2"
(3.8 cm)

handles (cut 2)
6" x 7/8" (15.2 x 2.2 cm)

Here's how

1 & 2 Cut squares of the faux leather, the lining fabric, and the iron-on adhesive. Next, follow the manufacturer's instructions to iron the adhesive onto the wrong side of the lining fabric square. Peel back the paper to expose the shiny adhesive.

3 With wrong sides together, iron the lining fabric/adhesive square to the faux-leather square. Be sure to iron the lining side, not the faux-leather side.

4 Using the dimensions at left, mark and cut the cross shape and the handles out of your laminated fabric. (Hint: A striped lining fabric makes measuring and cutting a breeze.)

5 At the point where the larger flap meets the smaller one, make a cut in the large flap perpendicular to its base. (See cutting instructions at left for length of cut.) This will be the portion that underlaps the front flap where the snaps will be.

6 Fit your machine with the leather needle. (See Specialty Sewing Machine Needles on page 13.) Use heavyweight thread if you want the topstitching to really stand out. Starting at the flap cuts made in step 5, topstitch along the perimeter about 1/8 inch (0.3 cm) in from the edge. (See Topstitching on page 14.)

(Continued on page 90)

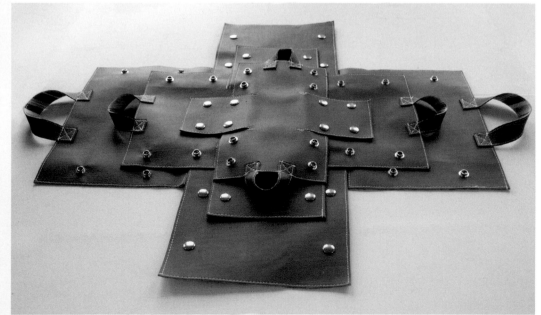

Here's how (continued)

7

8

9

10

11

12

7 Lay the piece flat in front of you, with the lining side up, the two shorter flaps at the top and bottom and the larger flaps on the left and right. The short flap closest to you will be the front. Start by folding up the larger flap on the left, then fold the smaller front flap up. The front flap will lap over the edge of the larger side flap by a couple of inches. Secure the two flaps together with a clothespin, as shown.

8 Now fold up the larger flap on the right side and lap its edge under the front flap as above. Secure with another clothespin. Repeat this folding and pinning for the back two corners.

9 You position the snaps where you like, or follow the dimensions I used:

For the LARGE BIN, the top snap is about $2^1/_2$ inches (6.4 cm) from the top and 1 inch (2.5 cm) from the edge. The second snap is about $6^1/_2$ inches (16.5 cm) down from the top edge.

For the MEDIUM BIN, the top snap is about $1^1/_2$ inches (3.8 cm) from the top and 1 inch (2.5 cm) from the edge. The second snap is about $4^1/_2$ inches (11.4 cm) down from the top edge.

For the SMALL BIN, the top snap is about $1^1/_4$ inches (3.2 cm) from the top and $3/_4$ inch (1.9 cm) from the edge. The second snap is about 3 inches (7.6 cm) down from the top edge.

Once you have established the points where the snaps will go, use a pin to mark the spot, pushing it straight through all layers of fabric on both flaps, as shown in photo 9.

10 You'll need to mark the positions for the female and the male snap pieces on both flaps. (Hint: it's easy if you use the positioned pins from step 9.) Pull the pin out a little so you can mark the base of the shaft where it goes through the faux leather. Use any kind of marker since the dot will be under the snap and won't show on the finished product. With the pin still in place, look inside the bin to where the end of the pin comes out of the lining fabric on the inside flap. Again, mark your spot.

11 Follow the manufacturer's instructions for your snap application tool to apply the female snaps to the marked spots on the bin's front flap. Then apply the male snap part to the faux-leather side of the side flap. Repeat for all flaps and snaps.

12 Topstitch along the perimeter of the handle pieces about $1/_8$ inch (0.3 cm) in from the edge. Attach the handles to the sides of the bins with an X-box stitch. (See X-Reinforcement on page 13.)

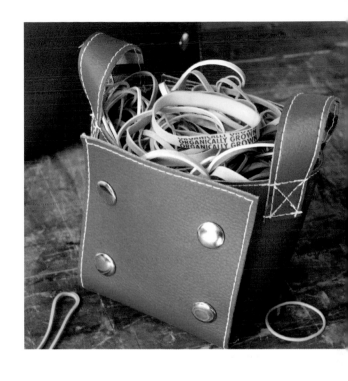

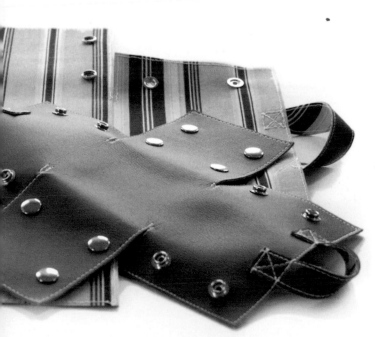

And when your bins are done storing things, they unsnap and fold flat so they can be easily stowed away. Pretty snappy!

EASE LEVEL:	*easy intermediate*

TIME REQUIREMENT:	*a nice morning project*

COST:	*real cheap for real furniture*

Ready-to-Roll MAT

Take some of the hard knocks out of your morning Pilates. Or roll out this mat for an oh-so-inviting afternoon siesta or a great impromptu sleepover pad for overflow guests. It even has a built-in headrest that does double duty. Roll up the pad and wrap the headrest around it, and you have a striking bolster cushion that is thoroughly at home on a sofa or a bed or a window seat.

Materials & Tools

- basic tool kit (see page 9)

- 2 yards (1.8 m) of medium- to heavyweight linen, cotton, or flax fabric, at least 54 inches (137.2 cm) wide for the mat

- 1 yard (0.9 m) of dupioni silk, fine linen, or something else scrumptious for the headrest, at least 45 inches (114.3 cm) wide

- 100 percent cotton quilt batting, enough for two or three layers, 30 x 96 inches (76.2 x 243.8 cm) for both the pad and the headrest

- embroidery floss, thin yarn, or heavyweight thread

- large-eyed needle

- hook-and-loop tape

Make the cut

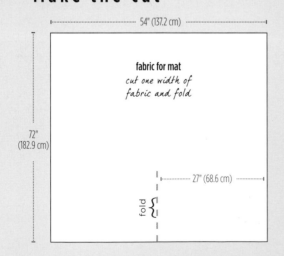

fabric for mat
cut one width of fabric and fold

54" (137.2 cm)

72" (182.9 cm)

27" (68.6 cm)

fold

36" (91.4 cm)

headrest
cut one piece and fold

36" (91.4 cm)

fold

6" (15.2 cm)

36" (91.4 cm) or less

fold

closure tab
cut one and fold

Sew it up

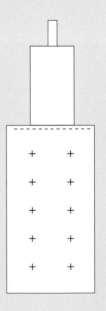

You can get the headrest and the tab closure out of 1 yard (0.9 m) of fabric by cutting the excess off the width to get your 36-inch (91.4 cm) square, then cutting the tab closure out of that excess (which is already the correct length).

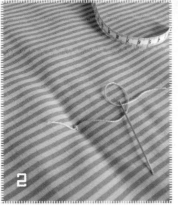

Here's how

1 Cut fabric to sizes specified at left. To make the mat, fold the fabric in half the long way with right sides together. Lay two layers (or three for extra cushiness) of 100 percent cotton quilt batting on the fabric, and pin through all the layers of fabric and batting. Sew a 1/2 inch (1.3 cm) seam around the perimeter on the long open side and the bottom (no need to sew the folded edge). Leave the top edge open. Trim the seam, and turn the entire mat so the right sides are outside and the batting is encased within. Finish the top edge by folding about 1/2 inch (1.3 cm) of the fabric to the inside. Machine-sew the top edge closed.

2 Use the embroidery floss or thin yarn threaded on the large-eyed needle to make square knot ties that go through all layers of the quilt to keep the batting from shifting. Make two rows of ties about 10 inches (25.4 cm) apart.

3 For the headrest, repeat step 1, but use only one or two layers of the cotton batting. Sew, trim, and turn, then finish the top edge just as in step 1.

4 Put the headrest piece on top of the mat, with the top edges even. Sew together with one row of topstitching. (See Topstitching on page 14.) Now, roll up the mat and wrap the headrest around the outside. Measure the distance around the roll, and add 8 inches (20.3 cm). Cut the fabric strip for your tab closure to that length.

5 To make the tab closure, fold the fabric in half, right sides together, to make a long strip. Pin and sew 1/2 inch (1.3 cm) in from the edge. Now fold the sewn piece so the new seam is centered down the middle of the long strap. From this centered seam, draw a 45° line angled down to the tab edge in both directions. Sew along these marked lines and then trim the excess to make the angled end of the strap. Turn the strap so it's right side out and tuck the raw ends in about 1/2 inch (1.3 cm), and pin. Press flat. Topstitch around the perimeter about 1/8 inch (0.3 cm) in from the edge, sewing the open end closed.

6 Position the finished tab closure so it's centered side-to-side on the headrest and the angled tongue extends about 3 inches (7.6 cm) beyond the headrest's edge as shown. Pin and sew in place with a 2-inch square (5.1 cm) of topstitching that runs right up to the edge of the headrest and down each side of the tab.

7 With the mat rolled up, wrap the tab closure around the headrest. Position a 1-inch (2.5 cm) square of hook-and-loop tape on the ends of the tab so it will close the roll snugly. Pin and sew the hook-and-loop tape pieces in place.

EASE LEVEL:	super simple
TIME REQUIREMENT:	a little more than an hour
COST:	frugal-friendly
PRACTICALITY FACTOR:	very high

Upholstery Webbing
BULLETIN BOARD

Life is three-dimensional, so why do most bulletin boards limit you to only two-dimensional things that can be run through with a tack? This bulletin board uses jute upholstery webbing to create pockets that can hold a rotating display of all the artifacts of your rich and busy life. The simple materials— jute, rough cotton, raw wood—seem both natural and industrial at the same time.

Materials & Tools

- basic tool kit (see page 9)

- 3/4 yard (68.6 cm) of natural canvas, linen, or (as shown here) inexpensive osnaburg cotton

- 3/4 yard (68.6 cm) of muslin

- 3/4 yard (68.6 cm) of medium-weight iron-on interfacing

- iron

- about 3 yards (2.7 m) of 3 1/2 inch (8.9 cm) wide jute upholstery webbing

- thread

- right triangle drafting tool (optional)

- foam board, 20 x 30-inch (50.8 x 76.2 cm)

- 1 stick, dowel, or bamboo pole, 28 to 40 inches (71.1 to 101.6 cm)

- jute string

Cut and sew

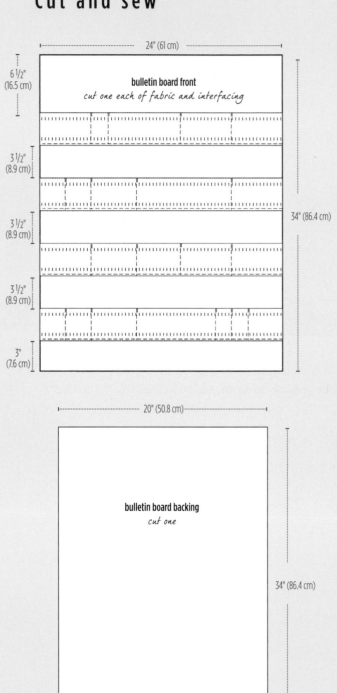

24" (61 cm)

6 ½" (16.5 cm)

bulletin board front
cut one each of fabric and interfacing

3 ½" (8.9 cm)

3 ½" (8.9 cm)

34" (86.4 cm)

3 ½" (8.9 cm)

3" (7.6 cm)

20" (50.8 cm)

bulletin board backing
cut one

34" (86.4 cm)

Here's how

To Start Cut the pieces of canvas, linen, or cotton for the front, the muslin for the back, and the interfacing, as per cutting instructions at left. Iron the interfacing to the front fabric, as per manufacturer's instructions.

1 Cut four pieces of upholstery webbing, each piece measuring 24 inches (61 cm) in length. Measure and mark position lines on the front fabric, as shown on the diagram at left. Pin the jute webbing into place.

2 Sew the webbing with a straight stitch about $^1/_8$ inch (0.3 cm) from the bottom edge of each pocket. Repeat for the remaining three pieces of jute.

3 Using the right triangle drafting tool (or really anything that has a right-angle edge), draw the divisions you'd like in your pockets anywhere from about 2 inches (5.2 cm) to 9 or 10 inches (22.9 or 25.4 cm) apart and then sew. (If they're any wider, you'll end up with gaping pockets.) Be sure to do a robust backtack at the top of each pocket ($^1/_2$ inch [1.3 cm] or so, two or three times back and forth) to reinforce the pocket edge.

4 & 5 With right sides together, pin the backing fabric to the front along the sides. Because the backing fabric is narrower than the front fabric, the front will be pulled around the edges to the back to form a nice, tidy finished edge. Sew the side seams, and turn the fabric right side out. Make sure the backing is centered, with about 1 inch (2.5 cm) of the front fabric wrapping around each side. Iron flat.

6 For the bottom hem, fold the fabric up about $^1/_2$ inch (1.3 cm), then fold up again until the edge of the fold is a scant 1/4 inch (0.6 cm) above the bottom edge of the bottommost pocket. Pin, and work all the way across. You're going to sew the hem along the same stitching line as the stitching from step 2. Transfer the pins to the front side of the fabric, and sew along the bottom edge of the pocket to secure the hem.

7 Slide the foam board into the interior.

8 To create the rod pocket at the top, fold down the top edge $^1/_2$ inch (1.3 cm), then fold it over again 2 to 2 $^1/_2$ inches (5.2 to 6.4 cm) and pin on the front side. Secure with a line of straight stitching close to the folded edge, being sure to capture all the fabric layers but staying clear of the foam board. Slide your stick or rod into the pocket, and suspend with jute string.

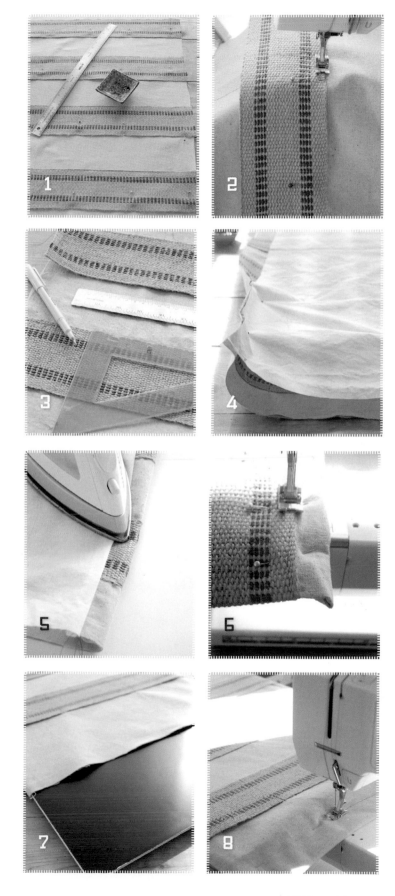

Pile-it-On DENIM RUG

Let your hands do something nice for your feet. This project takes a rough-and-tumble material, renowned for its ruggedness, and encourages it to embrace its softer side. Your sewing machine gets a workout, sewing dozens of diagonal lines through layers of fabric. But when the fabric is cut and the edges start fraying, this luscious little beauty blooms beneath your feet.

Materials & Tools

- basic tool kit (see page 9)
- 3 yards (2.7 m) of denim
- lots of thread
- washing machine/dryer
- stiff bristle brush (optional)

EASE LEVEL:	straight-sewing beginner
TIME REQUIREMENT:	a couple of hours
COST:	denim is cheap so layer it on!

Make the cut

20" (50.8 cm)

rug
cut six

30" (76.2 cm)

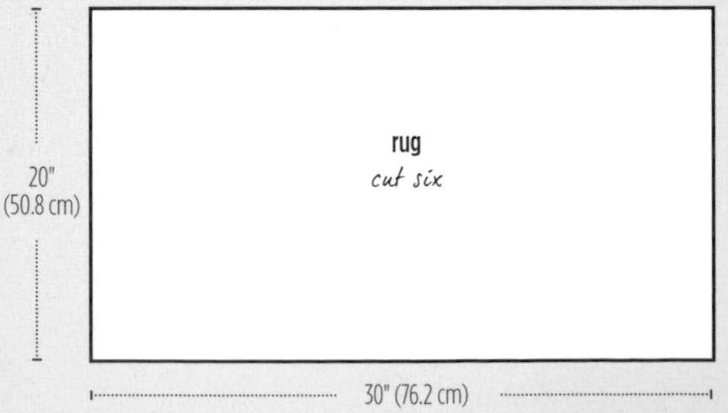

Here's how

1 Preshrink your denim in the washer and dryer. Then use the scissors and long straightedge to cut the six pieces of denim to size, as per cutting instructions at left. Layer them atop one another with right sides faceup. Pin in a few random places to secure.

2 With the yardstick and fabric pencil, mark a diagonal line from one corner of the fabric to another.

3 Draw lines, parallel to the first line, at 3/4 inch (1.9 cm) intervals until they cover all of the fabric area.

4 Use the pins to secure the layered fabrics together, then start machine-sewing down the marked lines. Be patient, go slow, and take out the pins before you run over them. Clip threads as you go (so you don't end up with a messy tangle). There are a lot of lines, but don't despair. It won't actually take that long, and you can always take a much-needed tea-and-biscuit break occasionally.

5 Whew, lines all sewn!

6 Use your sharpest scissors. Beginning at the edge, start cutting the fabric between the rows of stitching. Cut down through the top five layers of fabric, leaving the base layer intact. Because denim is thick and tough, you'll probably be able to cut through only one or two layers at a time. This step, therefore, is also a chance to go slow, stop rushing, and meditate on making the earth a softer, cushier place.

7 The fabric layers move a little in the sewing process. Mark a straight line along each side of the rectangle, and cut.

8 To keep the edges of the rug tidy after all the fraying and fluffing, sew a line of stitching around the perimeter of the rug about 1/4 inch (0.6 cm) in from the edge. Now toss the rug in the washer—preferably with a load of jeans—so the friction can really bring up the "bloom" of the frayed fabric. Put in a hot dryer, also with some other clothes, so that it has plenty to rub up against as it tumbles. Be sure to check the lint screen about halfway through the drying process. Remove, and rub the rug against itself to bring up even more bloom. If you'd like, use a stiff bristled brush to cause even more blooming and fraying.

give it away!

Conical Coin Purse

Laminated Felt Case

Inner Tube Day Planner • Sew-Green Gift Tags • Selvage-Striped Tote

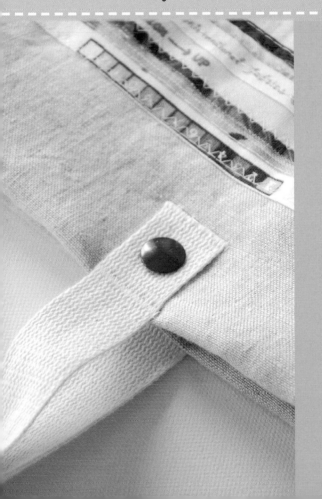

EASE LEVEL:	*embarrassingly easy*
TIME REQUIREMENT:	*literally 15 minutes!*
COST:	*c'mon, a zipper and some ribbon?*
CUMULATIVE EFFECT:	*will make you grin*

Conical COIN PURSE

The physics of sewing is sometimes so magical. A tiny bit of structural engineering can take a flat, two-dimensional piece of material and make it bloom into a three-dimensional, useable, wearable object that others are sure to covet. Here's an excellent example: with just a twist, this little utilitarian coin purse jumps off the page. It's a simple equation that's open to a thousand variations. Try it in felt or in inner tube rubber!

Materials & Tools

- basic tool kit (see page 9)

- 1$^1/_2$ yard (1.4 m) of grosgrain ribbon, 1$^1/_2$ inches (3.8 cm) wide

- sewing machine with both a zigzag stitch and a zipper foot or needle that can be adjusted side to side

- one 4-inch (10.2 cm) nylon zipper (can be cut to length from longer one)

- scrap of contrasting ribbon for tie (optional)

Make the cut

There is no magic number here. You can make this little purse any size you want. However, if it's much smaller than 4 inches (10.2 cm) on a side, it'll be hard to get your fingers into. If it's too big, it loses some of its charm. To make the one shown here, use the measurements below.

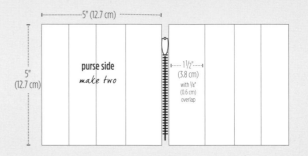

To make the purse easier to open and carry, thread a piece of contrasting ribbon through the hole in the zipper pull. Cutting the ribbon end on an angle makes it easier to start it through. For a little knotted fob like this one, you'll need about 6 inches (15.2 cm). For a wristlet handle (shown on page 105), start with about 18 inches (45.7 cm), then knot and trim to your liking.

Here's how

1 Cut eight pieces of the 1 1/2-inch-wide (3.8 cm) grosgrain ribbon, each piece 5 inches (12.7 cm) long.

2 Pin four pieces of ribbon together, overlapping the edges by 1/4 inch (0.6 cm). Machine-sew together along the edge of each ribbon, making sure to catch the ribbon beneath it. Repeat, sewing together the other four pieces of ribbon.

3 Since 4-inch (10.2 cm) zippers are hard to find in interesting colors, it's often easier to buy a longer zipper and cut it to length. Measure down 4 inches (10.2 cm) on your zipper and mark. Using a tight zigzag stitch (so tight, the stitches sew right on top of each other), sew across the bottom of the zipper at the marked point, as shown. This will be the new "stop" on the zipper.

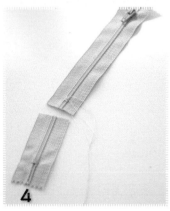

4 Cut the zipper off about 1/2 inch (1.3 cm) from the stitching point.

5 Butt the long, uncut side of the ribbon almost to the zipper teeth, and pin into place. Baste the zipper in place. Repeat the process on the zipper's other side.

6 Use a zipper foot or position the machine's needle to the far left. Sew about 1/8 inch (0.3 cm) in from the ribbon edge as shown. Stop the sewing halfway, and close the zipper so you don't have to sew past the zipper pull, resulting in a wobbly stitch line. Repeat on the zipper's other side.

7 Open the zipper before continuing. Fold along the zipper, right sides facing, to make a square pouch. Pin and sew a 1/2 inch (1.3 cm) seam along the bottom and one of the sides. Finish the raw edges of these seams with a zigzag stitch to keep them from fraying.

8 Here's the magic moment: You're not going to simply seam the third side as is. Instead, fold the unseamed edge in the opposite direction, so the two existing seams meet in the middle. Pin, then sew this final seam, and finish with a zigzag as before. Turn the purse right-side out through the open zipper.

EASE LEVEL:	shallow learning curve
TIME REQUIREMENT:	finish it in one sitting
COST:	cheaper than gas
UNEXPECTED MATERIALS:	fusible adhesive
UNUSUAL TOOLS:	leather needle

Laminated FELT CASE

Every gewgaw in its place. For the person who has lots of gadgets, here is the perfect case to keep a small music player or cell phone safe from the hard knocks of life. Made from a scrumptious palette of layered and fused wool felt, this quirky, multicolored case comes together in a wink and is guaranteed to bring a grin.

Materials & Tools

- basic tool kit (see page 9)

- 3 pieces of wool felt (or wool/rayon blend), each 12 inches (30.5 cm) square, in brown, lime green, and dark green, *or* 1/4 yard (22.9 cm) of each color

- 1 piece of wool felt (or wool/rayon blend), 18 inches (45.7 cm) square, in white or cream, *or* 1/4 yard (22.9 cm)

- iron

- 1/2 yard (45.7 cm) of fusible adhesive (make sure it's "sew-able" adhesive)

- hole punch

- very sharp scissors or a rotary cutter

- leather needle (for the sewing machine)

- 1 cool button

- about 12 inches (30.5 cm) of elastic cord

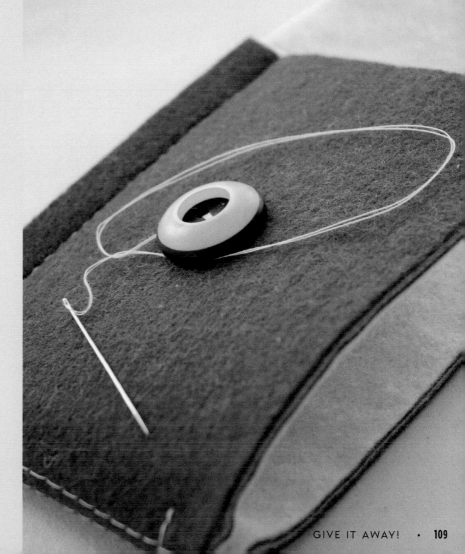

Make the cut

These instructions make a case that measures $3^1/_2$ x 5 inches (8.9 x 12.7 cm). It fits a slim music player perfectly. If you'd like to make a case for a larger gadget, measure the object and then add 2 inches (5.1 cm) to both its height and width.

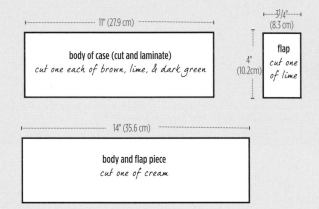

11" (27.9 cm)

body of case (cut and laminate)
cut one each of brown, lime, & dark green

3|/4"
(8.3 cm)

4"
(10.2cm)

flap
*cut one
of lime*

14" (35.6 cm)

body and flap piece
cut one of cream

Put it together

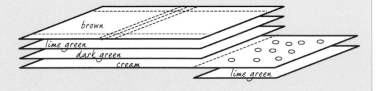

brown

lime green

dark green

cream

lime green

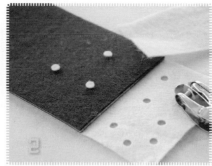

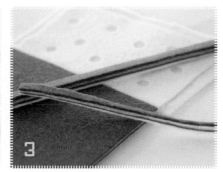

Here's how

1 Cut the felt pieces, as per instructions at left. Follow the manufacturer's instructions to iron the adhesive onto the brown felt rectangle. Continue alternating adhesive and felt as you add the lime green, the dark green, and finally the cream felt rectangles. Because the cream rectangle is longer than the others, you'll line up the bottom edges of all layers and let the cream overhang to make the flap.

2 Use the hole punch to make random holes in the cream flap. Fuse the lime green flap to the backside of the cream-colored flap.

3 Now that all layers are fused together, use sharp scissors or a rotary cutter to cut $1/4$ inch (0.6 cm) off all sides. This will make the edges clean and show off the different strata of color.

4 Mark the center of the brown felt piece, and sew a line of stitching across the rectangle at that point to serve as the fold line; it'll make folding the thick fabric much easier. Add two more lines of stitching about $1/8$ inch (0.3 cm) on either side of the first.

5 Fold the rectangle (wrong/cream sides together) along the lines of stitching and line up the sides. Sew about $1/2$ inch (1.3 cm) from the edge down both sides to make the case. You'll be going through lots of layers here, but if you use a leather needle (see Specialty Sewing Machine Needles on page 13) and sew very slowly, it should go quite smoothly.

6 Sew on the button you've chosen about $3^1/2$ inches (8.9 cm) from the case's top edge. Poke two small holes through the felt near the case's top edge on the opposite side. Next, cut an 8-inch (20.3 cm) length piece of elastic cord, and thread it through the two holes, with the loose ends to the inside. Tie loosely, fold the flap down, and stretch the elastic loop down over the button to close. Adjust the length if necessary before pulling the knot tight. Cut the ends of the elastic close to the knot.

EASE LEVEL:	gutsy beginner
TIME REQUIREMENT:	60 minutes tops
COST:	dirt cheap
UNEXPECTED MATERIALS:	colored elastic
UNUSUAL TOOLS:	leather needle

Check with your local tire dealer to find an inner tube. Tire shops often have a stack of old inner tubes by the dumpster that they would be happy to see put to a better use.

Inner Tube DAY PLANNER

Who would have thought that such a sophisticated and urbane use could be found for an old tire inner tube? The rubber is actually quite beautiful once you liberate it from its gritty, road-weary existence. The surface has a complex color and texture with a lovely patina not unlike aged leather. But it's oh-so-much-more eco-friendly! If recycled rubber isn't your thing, make these with leather, patent leather, or oilcloth.

Materials & Tools

- basic tool kit (see page 9)

- one truck tire inner tube

- address book, notebook, checkbook or datebook calendar

- craft/household scissors (for the inner tube)

- sewing scissors (for the fabric)

- 1/4 yard (22.9 cm) of lining fabric

- iron-on interfacing (about 1/4 yard [22.9 cm])

- iron

- double-stick tape

- leather needle

- length of colored elastic, 1/4 to 1/2-inch (0.6 to 1.3 cm) wide by 12 to 18 inches (30.5 to 45.7 cm) long

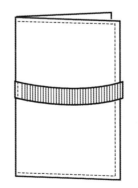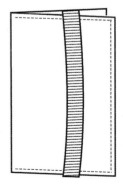

There are two ways to close the agenda cover. You can make a loop of elastic that goes horizontally around the center of cover. Or you can send the elastic vertically over the top of the cover and sew it in between the inner tube and the lining. Hey, it's your thing. Do what you want to do....

Black or white elastic is easy to find, but getting your hands on some technicolor elastic might be a stretch. Colored elastics are often used in bathing suits, lingerie, and costumes (like for figure skaters), so you can look for websites that carry supplies for those specialties. I found mine (in cherry red and lime green) at a big-city fabric store. It was way down deep on a lower shelf and marked "swimsuit elastic." Check the resource list at larkbooks.com for more ideas.

Make the cut

For the lining fabric, iron on a medium-weight interfacing to the wrong side of the fabric. This will make the fabric firmer and keep the edges from fraying, so you can leave them raw.

Cut the main piece from the interfaced lining fabric. Cut two pieces from the interfaced lining fabric for flaps. Cut one main piece from the inner tube.

main piece
size of open book plus 1" (2.5 cm)
on all sides
cut one

main lining/interfacing piece
size of open book plus 1"
(2.5 cm) on all sides
cut one of each

flaps
lining/interfacing
1/4 width of
main piece
cut two

flap | lining fabric | flap

elastic

Here's how

1 After washing and drying the inner tube, "harvest" the rubber. Cut a piece of the tube that's big enough to cover your open planner, agenda, or checkbook, with at least an inch (2.5 cm) to spare all the way around. (See the cutting diagram at left.)

2 Iron the interfacing onto the lining's wrong side, and then cut pieces of interfaced fabric, using the cutting diagrams at left. Fold the piece in half to make spine.

3 Cut flaps out of the interfaced fabric, and position along the outside edges of lining fabric. Tape into place.

4 With wrong sides together, tape the lining onto the inner tube rubber piece using double-stick tape (or use a rolled piece of single-sided tape). If you are choosing to have the elastic run vertically on your cover, cut a piece of elastic that is the height of your cover, and tuck the ends in between the inner tube and the lining fabric.

5 Fit your machine with a leather sewing needle. (See Specialty Sewing Machine Needles on page 13.) Sew all the way around the perimeter of the fabric and rubber about 1/4 inch (0.6 cm) from the edge.

6 Measure to the center of the fabric and sew a vertical line of stitching to create a "spine." This will train the book cover to fold gracefully along its center.

7 Use sharp craft scissors to trim around the perimeter, about 1/8 inch (0.3 cm) from the stitching.

8 Measure a loop of elastic that stretches a little when it goes around the book's middle. Add about 1/2 inch (1.3 cm) to the length to allow for the seam in the elastic. Overlap the ends of the elastic to create a loop, and sew them together with a zigzag stitch. Tape the seam of the loop into the center of the book's spine, and sew into position with a straight stitch.

Now you're ready to slip the contents (calendar, address book, checkbook, or notebook) into the flaps of your sewn cover, as shown below.

Sew-Green GIFT TAGS

Don't spend any more of your hard-earned money on boring, anonymous gift tags that say nothing but "ho hum" for the holidays. Get cryptic, get clever, get crafty; sew up your own, using eco-friendly scraps of paper.

Materials & Tools

- basic tool kit (see page 9)
- old magazines
- pinking shears (optional)
- random sheets of colored cardstock
- glue stick
- regular or heavyweight thread
- jute or hemp string
- hole punch (optional)

Here's how

1 To make the labels, cut out fun words and piquant slogans from the old magazines.

2 Cut out labels in various shapes from the colored cardstock paper.

3 Position the words on the cardstock tags. Attach them with a tiny dot of glue in the center. Using regular or heavyweight thread, machine-sew the words into place, outlining the clippings with a straight or zigzag stitch. Add additional decorative stitching as you like.

4 Sew a loop of jute or hemp string in place at the top of the tag, using a tight zigzag stitch. Alternatively, you can punch a hole in the tag and loop string through it to make a convenient way to attach tags to their packages.

EASE LEVEL: *simple skill set*

TIME REQUIREMENT: *2 hours or fewer*

COST: *raid your fabric stash!*

CLAIM TO FAME: *embellishment with an edge*

Selvage-Striped TOTE

Written in the margins of just about every piece of fabric is information. The selvages are part of the printing process and contain names, numbers, manufacturers, and printing graphics like color bars and registration marks. These marks appear only on fabrics that are printed with designs, so if you're looking for interesting selvages, printed cottons, home-dec fabrics, and printed flannels are good candidates.

Materials & Tools

- basic tool kit (see page 9)

- 1 yard (0.9 m) of linen, canvas, or cotton duck

- 1 yard (0.9 m) of lining fabric

- 1¹/₂ yards (1.4 m) of natural colored webbing for straps, about 1 inch (2.5 cm) wide (for tote)

- dozens of strips of selvedge material cut from fabrics in your stash

- foam pillow insert (if you're making a pillow; see page 123)

- 4 buttons, rivets, or grommets (for the tote)

Make the cut

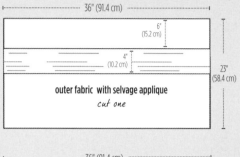

36" (91.4 cm)

6" (15.2 cm)

4" (10.2 cm)

23" (58.4 cm)

outer fabric with selvage applique
cut one

36" (91.4 cm)

lining fabric
cut one

21" (53.3 cm)

20–24" (50.8 – 61 cm)

straps (cut 2)
Straps that are 20 to 24 inches (50.8 to 61 cm) long are a good length; they can be worn over the shoulder or held in your hand. Sew them on the bag, as shown below, with strap ends placed about 1 1/2 inch (3.8 cm) down from the bag's top edge, centered, and about 8 inches (20.3 cm) apart.

Put it together

1 1/2" (3.8 cm)

8" (20.3 cm)

to make bottom gusset
follow the instructions in Step 8

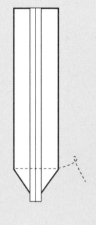

Here's how

1 After prewashing all the materials, cut out the pieces of fabric, lining, and webbing, as per cutting instructions at left. Raid your fabric stash, and look along the edges for interesting printed selvedges. Cut the selvages off the fabric, taking a little of the edge of the fabric as well.

2 Using a long straightedge and a fabric marker, mark an area, starting about 6 inches (15.2 cm) down from the top, that will be filled with the appliquéd selvages. For the tote, I created an area about 5 inches (12.7 cm) wide that ran the length of the fabric.

3 Begin by laying out one selvage strip along the appliqué area's bottom edge. Pin, then machine-sew with either a straight stitch or a zigzag. This is not a project for those who have any fray-phobias. It's expected that to achieve the appropriate level of edgy funk, there will be frays.

4, 5, & 6 Continue adding strips of selvage, overlapping each piece a little over the previous one until the entire area is covered. I used a combination of both zigzag and straight stitches for appliquéing the selvage strips. If you have a long, blank portion of selvage, you can add a short strip of something more interesting in the middle of it, stitching the shorter piece right over the other selvage.

(continued on page 122)

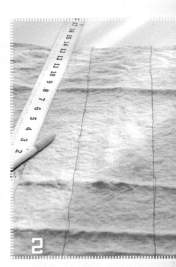

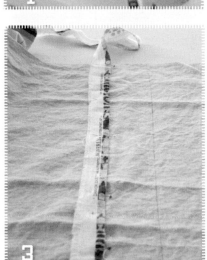

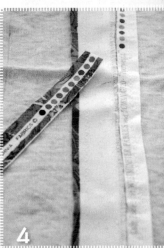

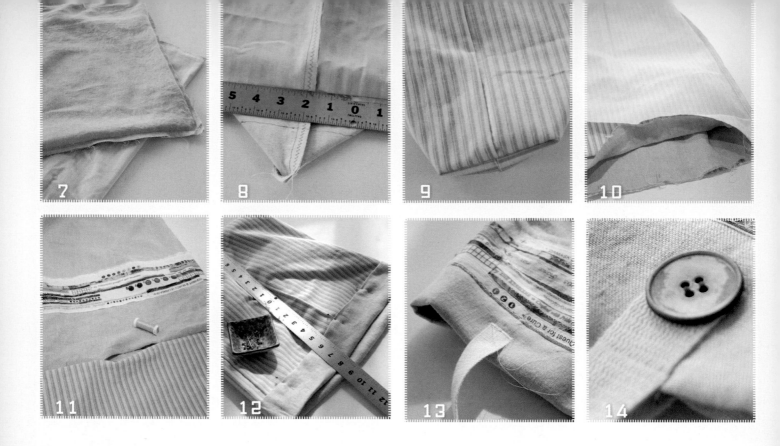

7 To make the tote, take the outer fabric and lining pieces, and fold each of them in half the long way (right sides facing). Pin and sew a $1/2$ inch (1.3 cm) seam along one side and the bottom of the outer fabric to form a bag. Repeat for the lining.

8 At the outer fabric bag's bottom corner, open up the corner so the seam is centered and the corner is pointing downward, as shown. Draw a horizontal line about $2^1/2$ inches (6.4 cm) up from the corner point. Sew along this line to make the bag's bottom gusset. Repeat on the other corner (even though there's no seam on that side). Then repeat the whole process on the lining.

9 Photo 9 shows what the gusset looks like when turned right side out. See how it creates a "bottom" for the bag?

10 Turn the outer fabric bag right side out and the lining fabric bag right side in. Put the outer fabric bag inside the lining fabric bag; line up the top edges and side seams of each, and pin. Sew a $1/2$-inch (1.3 cm) seam along the top edge to connect the two. Leave a 3-inch (7.6 cm) gap open to turn the bags.

11 Turn the bag through the gap so right sides are out. Hand sew the gap closed. Stuff the lining fabric down into the outer bag until the bottoms are touching. Because the lining fabric is shorter than the outer, there will be a "hem" of outer fabric at the top. Now, turn the bag inside out.

12 To give the tote more body and strength, fold down the top edge 2 to $2^1/2$ inches (5.1 to 6.4 cm) toward the bag's inside to make a cuff. The cuff's edge should line up on the inside to the place where the top of the appliqué area falls on the outside. Pin in place to hold, and then turn the bag right side out and re-pin on the outside. Sew along the top edge of the appliqué area, catching the edge of the cuff on the inside.

13 See the diagram on page 120 for the placement and length of the straps. Attach them with a tight zigzag along the bottom edge of the strap and the top edge of the tote.

14 Sew another row of tight zigzag across the strap at the top edge of the bag. Then attach the button, rivet, or grommet accent (see Grommets on page 13) to finish off your tote with style.

Would you rather make an edgy pillow with your selvaged fabric? Simply cut the fabric to the size of your pillow, and add 2 inches (5.1 cm) each way for the seams and the thickness of the pillow. Then make a pillow back similar to the one used on page 82, so it's easy to remove the pillow insert for washing.

SLIPPER BOOTS

PHOTOCOPY AT

200% for woman's shoe sizes 6-7

205% for sizes 8-9

210% for size 10 and up

boot top BACK

cut two of outer fabric
cut six of lining fabric

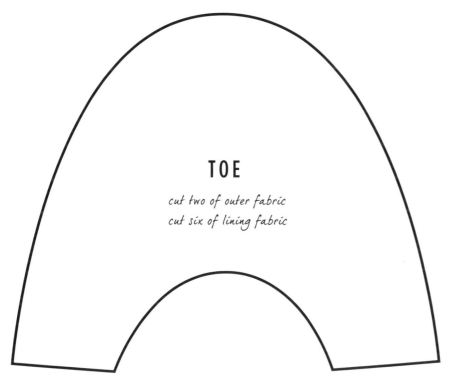

TOE

cut two of outer fabric
cut six of lining fabric

SLIPPER BOOT PATTERN PIECES

Photocopy pattern pieces at the enlargement appropriate to your shoe size. Cut out the pieces as per the instructions on page 46. The pattern piece for the "outer sole" is illustrated here with the dotted line within the sole pattern piece.

Seam allowance is included in all pattern pieces.

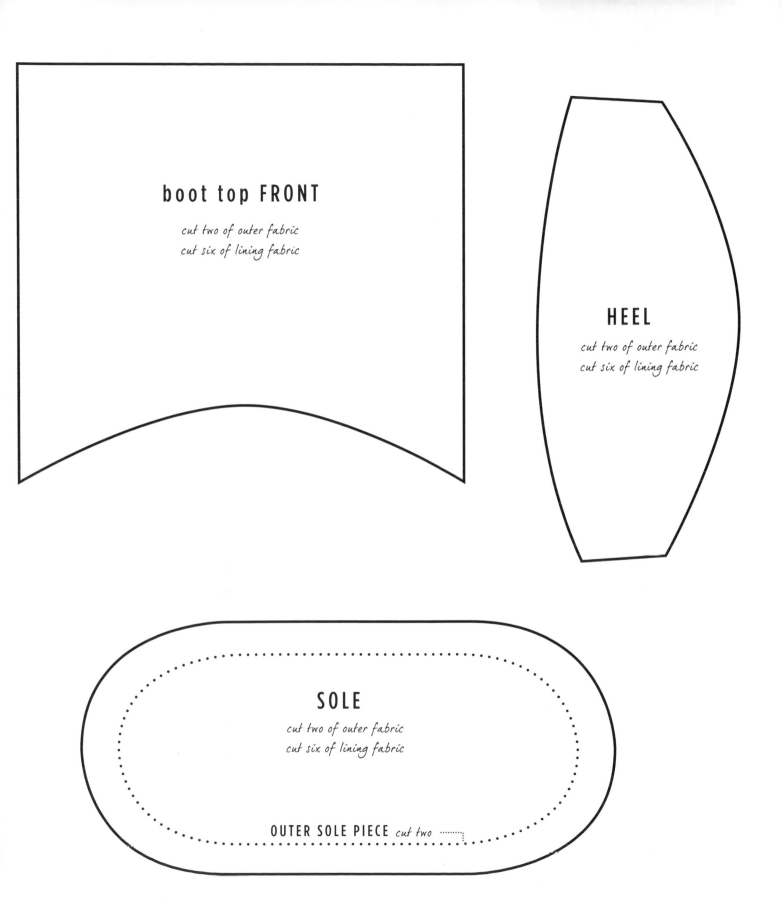

boot top FRONT

cut two of outer fabric
cut six of lining fabric

HEEL

cut two of outer fabric
cut six of lining fabric

SOLE

cut two of outer fabric
cut six of lining fabric

OUTER SOLE PIECE *cut two*

TRAPPER'S HAT

PHOTOCOPY AT 200%

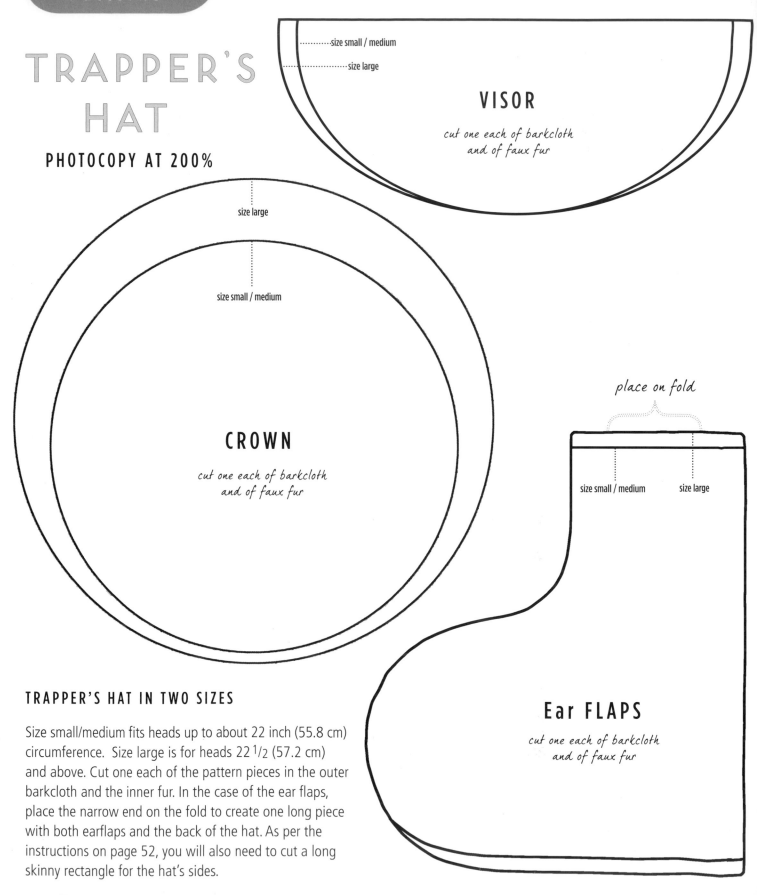

VISOR

*cut one each of barkcloth
and of faux fur*

size small / medium

size large

CROWN

*cut one each of barkcloth
and of faux fur*

size large

size small / medium

place on fold

size small / medium   size large

Ear FLAPS

*cut one each of barkcloth
and of faux fur*

TRAPPER'S HAT IN TWO SIZES

Size small/medium fits heads up to about 22 inch (55.8 cm) circumference. Size large is for heads 22 $1/2$ (57.2 cm) and above. Cut one each of the pattern pieces in the outer barkcloth and the inner fur. In the case of the ear flaps, place the narrow end on the fold to create one long piece with both earflaps and the back of the hat. As per the instructions on page 52, you will also need to cut a long skinny rectangle for the hat's sides.

ACKNOWLEDGMENTS

Books are funny creatures, long hours of solitary labor punctuated by dizzying flurries of brainstorming and collaborating. I am lucky to have an incredible family and friends as a constant source of inspiration. Their many hands make light work of the innumerable tasks that go into this busy life. I want to give thanks to my dearest dear Eliza Kuelthau who listened to a lot of moaning and cajoled me through a lot of doubting, giving freely of her insightful opinions and lending her lithe form to the projects within this book. Love and thanks to my darling daughter, Camille Wasinger, who was willing to test-drive the projects and then smile happily and beautifully for the camera. To my husband, Tom, who makes sure I get my sanity-protecting daily dose of mountain bike riding. To my son, Rainer, who is cool enough to know how to hit a clutch triple in the bottom of the ninth AND knit his own natty little ski hat.

Thanks to the wonderful folks at Lark Books—Valerie Shrader (who has a laugh that can cure all ills), Jane Harris Woodside, Chris Bryant, Nicole McConville, Paige Gilchrist, Meaghan Finnerty, and many others who know how to leave me alone and push me around in turns. What would I do without all of you?

And to my favorite feisty seamsters: Marlies Harris, Elizabeth Abplanalp, Gladys P. Harris, Margaret Williman Blatter, Julie Stutsman Garner, and Linda Ligon. And to my dear dad, Ronald Harris, who sewed a lovely dress for me when I was 4 years old, long before it was hip for guys to give such things a try. He appreciated sewing as a practical, beautiful application of engineering and physics, and he taught me to do the same.

INDEX

Appliqué, 10

Barkcloth, 51-55, 81

Buttons, 56-58

Carabiners, 30

Cuffs, 65

Denim, 100

Eco-felt, 19, 56-57

Elastic, 114

Faux Fur, 51-52

Felting, 69

Flannel, 45-46

Fleece, 61-62

Grommets, 13, 29, 77

Hardware, 13

Inner tube, 112-113

Inspiration, 14

Jute upholstery webbing, 81, 97

Laminating, 89

Lampshade, 77-79

Linen, 65, 93

Machines, 9

Materials, 10

Plastic shopping bags, 33

Reinforcement, 13

Seams, 11

Selvages, 119, 123

Sewing, 9

    Needles, 9, 13

    Pins, 9

    Presser foot, 9

Snaps, 14, 87

Stitches, 9, 14

    Crazy stitching, 14

    Topstitching, 14

Thread, 10

Tool kit, 9

T-shirts, 39, 71

Wool, 67

Zippers, 105